Parents Arise

"by a composer of Children Arise Scripture in song"

JANINE TARGETT

Balboa Press books may be ordered through booksellers or by contacting:

Balboa Press
A Division of Hay House
1663 Liberty Drive
Bloomington, IN 47403
www.balboapress.com
1 (877) 407-4847

ISBN: 978-1-4525-3039-0 (sc)
ISBN: 978-1-4525-3038-3 (e)

Print information available on the last page.

Balboa Press rev. date: 10/02/2015

BALBOA PRESS
A DIVISION OF HAY HOUSE

Endorsements for the book Parents Arise.

It is a privilege to highly recommend Janine and Paul's book 'Parents Arise.' I have personally observed them weaving the truths of God's Word into the lives of their children through riveting stories and catchy melodies. Like golden threads that remain for a lifetime these verses have become a part of their lives and have been a source of wisdom, instruction and comfort. Join the growing army of families who desire to raise up children strong in the Lord and in the knowledge and application of His Word.

Merrilyn Billing. Senior Pastor Zions Hill Church. Launceston. Tasmania.

'Parents Arise' has given me the missing link in my parenting. It also provides the tools for acting on the learning immediately.

Karen. Tasmania. Australia.

What a beautiful and inspirational journal of a family that God will model in this needy day and age – because of your obedience and skill of sharing with refreshing honesty, humour and instruction! Janine, what a beautiful book you have produced – it is now SO important that you send it forth, in any way you can – it must get out there! What a beautiful gift He has given you to be able to record with practical reality which will be such a tool to relate to all families. Multitudes will use your family testimony and instruction to 'Parents Arise.'

Pauline. Tasmania. Australia

Janine, Oh what a blessing to receive your book 'Parents Arise.' It is excellent! I am so excited now about promoting it with our parents. You are a blessing to not just your family, but families all over this country and others too.

Joan. Perth. Western Australia.

Janine, I have just finished reading your wonderful book 'Parents Arise' that a friend sent me. It is such an easy read, so practical and I can't wait to put it into practice! I couldn't put it down when I was reading it! Thank you for obeying God's calling to write the book and thank you for your honesty in it.

Jo. New Zealand.

I read 'Parents Arise' and was INSPIRED and CHALLENGED! It gave me confidence to read of a parent's testimony once their children have grown! God's Word works! Thank you for sharing.

Alexandra. Queensland. Australia.

Thank you Janine. The thing that struck me was the application of the memory work. There are a lot of systems out there to memorise Scripture and yet taking it to the next step and actually working it into our life is really what 'hiding God's Word in our heart' is all about. So it was excellent.

Caitlyn. Northern Territory. Australia.

Janine, I have just read your book from cover to cover tonight and couldn't put it down. I just wanted to thank you for being obedient to this and just for being you – so transparent, so beautiful inside and out and for reaching into the lives of so many and so many more to come. I was totally blessed and inspired.

Bronwyn. Tasmania. Australia.

Recently the leader of our mothers group bought your book 'Parents Arise.' I had the privilege to be the first to read it! Wow! I loved it so much I couldn't put it down. It confirmed what has been in my heart for some time about teaching my children Scriptures. I really loved and appreciated your journey through life so far. It is so simply written and easily able to identify with. You have done a wonderful job. I hope our church will in the future organise to run your course too. That would be awesome!

Sherrie. Tasmania. Australia.

Thank you for your book 'Parents Arise.' It was life changing!

Wendy. Queensland. Australia

Janine, I want to thank you for the copy of your inspiring book 'Parents Arise' and for being one of the major positive influences in my life. I wish you all the best as you continue to follow God's call to build strong, healthy families – it is so needed and I know that you are and will be a blessing to so many people.

Emma. Brisbane. Australia.

I have just finished your book! I must say it was ever so convicting and challenging and encouraging! Thank you! I do have a 'Verse Time' with the children BUT as time goes on I have let that time go or not been as consistent doing it as I once was. Thank you for the fresh reminder IT IS important and IT IS worth keeping on doing it. Thanks again Janine, the book was a good prompt to keep going and to refine even more, the work I am doing with my own family.

Mel. Tasmania. Australia.

Dear Readers, this is an amazing inspiring encouraging book! It is THAT good!

Heather Jones. Director of Above Rubies Ministries. New Zealand.

I loved reading the book. It has been an encouragement to us as a family. It is great to hear all those stories. Just shared tonight about Andrea's comment – 'Mum, I want to rebel' – but how she couldn't because God's Word was in her heart and she was convicted.

Claude. Victoria. Australia.

We've not done Verse Time before. Our kids have loved it and we're looking forward to continuing it as part of our weekly routine.

Louise. Tasmania. Australia.

THIS BOOK IS DEDICATED TO:

My amazing husband Paul. How can I ever thank you enough? You encourage and support my ideas and without you this book would never have happened. Our children and I love and respect you so much. You are a true example of a godly husband and father.

All my love always, Janine.

To Andrea, Jonathan and Michelle, thank you for being willing to allow me to share your stories with other families.

Special thanks to my editor, Megan Sayer for your hard work and invaluable suggestions. Thank you too, Murray Butwell, my page designer, and Val Stares, my final proof reader. Without you three this book might never have been completed.

Scripture quotations are taken from the King James version unless otherwise indicated. Scriptures marked (NIV) are from the New International Version and scriptures marked (LB) are from The Living Bible.

Note: Some Scriptures quoted below chapter headings also have the words, Children Arise Vol --- after them. These Scriptures have music composed to them and the Children Arise CDs can be ordered from www.parentsarise.com.au

Foreword

Jan and I were guest speakers at an *Above Rubies* Ladies camp held in Tasmania. I had, had the privilege of hearing a couple of the *Children Arise* CD's previously and loved them. However, my children were now grown, so I passed them on to mothers who were looking for a way to teach their children Scripture.

I had not heard of the story behind these wonderful CD's and when Jan shared her story we were all immensely blessed, and in turn encouraged to go out and 'do likewise'.

Jan is so very honest. She didn't make excuses for herself. She shared her faults along with her strengths, which is always an encouragement for those planning to follow her example.

This book is not just about teaching your children Scripture; it is so much more than that! It is a step by step walk with the Holy Spirit. It is about walking in faith and allowing God to reveal strategies pertinent to the situation at hand. It is about God being central in their lives as individuals and as a family. Jan testifies how she was guided through each trial. Through her obedience Jan was able to teach her children God's ways for life in a way that they could understand and receive.

Nothing works like standing on the Word of God! Over and over again Jan proves and testifies to the power, the truth and the hope found in His Word.

May God's hand of blessing be upon every parent as they set their hearts to prepare and teach their children God's ways for life.

Val Stares

Director *Above Rubies Australia.*

CONTENTS

Introduction

"Do not merely listen to the Word and so deceive yourselves, do what it says!"

James 1.22. (NIV) Children Arise Vol 4

Why have I chosen this verse to begin the story of our family? This past week has been an interesting time. God has spoken very clearly to me in many ways. A few days ago I came home to find a beautiful verse from Children Arise Volume 4 was playing loudly from one end of the house. The sound of sweet children's voices sang: *"Do not merely listen to the Word and so deceive yourselves, Do what it says!"*

My first thought was "who turned on the C.D. player?" and, when I realised there had been no one in the house for the last two hours, some prickles went up my spine. My next question was "why THAT verse?"

When Paul arrived home that night I asked him if he had been playing the Children Arise CD before he went to work, but he shook his head. What was that all about?

Two days later in church, our worship leader began to sing prophetically, and he found himself singing over and over again - guess what? *"Do not merely listen to the Word and so deceive yourselves, do what it says!"*

After singing this verse over and over for some time he finally finished, opened his eyes and, out of a congregation of perhaps one hundred and fifty people, looked straight at me. Again I was puzzled. What was God saying?

A day later, while cleaning out a drawer which hadn't been sorted for some time I pulled out a scrap of paper that my sister Merrilyn Billling had written on six years before. It said, NEEN! IT'S TIME TO WRITE A BOOK! I knew the story was in me, but I had not brought it out on paper.

Through the week God continued to be on my case. I was looking for a new C.D cover to replace a broken one, when I opened a drawer filled with Above Rubies magazines and some letters from women around the world responding to an article I'd written ten years before. As I placed my hand upon the precious letters and magazines I began to cry – LOUDLY - and I couldn't stop! What was going on? I sat and cried, and grieved, for twenty minutes or so. I wondered how I had allowed my life to become so busy and so focused on other things that I no longer had time for the dream God had placed in my heart many years before - the dream to share with other mothers the wonderful story God had given me to tell.

That night I couldn't sleep. Finally at two in the morning I made myself a cup of tea, and sat in our lounge room to inquire of the Lord. "Lord, what is going on? What are you trying to tell me?" I sat with my pen and paper in hand and began to write. Thoughts flowed effortlessly, and my pen was racing over the pages. An hour later, when I read what had come to mind, I had a clear request from God to take six months and write down the story of our family. He reminded me that He had asked me many times in the past, and had even confirmed it through people like my faithful sister. I had ignored the request and continued to become busier and busier with other things. He was now very clearly asking me again, and I was impressed that the time limit was six months. This meant that when our beautiful twin girls Ava and Jessica, our 10th and 11th Grandchildren turned one on 31st August, the copy would be completed. I now understood why I had cried and grieved the night before. There was a story to tell and it had remained a dream that was locked up tightly inside me. Being reminded of my article had opened the door to this dream that had been locked up for so long. There was a story that needed to be told, and my hearts desire was that other mothers could be encouraged to teach and train their children in God's ways too.

I now understood the puzzling visit of a very good friend and prophetic prayer warrior a month before. She told Paul and I that God had clearly shown her that He had plans for us both, and, while there had been an open door in the past, it was now almost shut, but God had his foot in the doorway and would not allow it to shut completely. She told us there would be much opposition to what He was leading us into, and some would even come from within the Church. She said there was already a strong force against the door to close it. I realized the 'open door' was the opportunity to share with other parents what we had learned in our own family life, and I felt that this was my final opportunity to write it down.

Over the years God gave our family some amazing keys to life and the further we delved into Scriptures, sang them, and put them into practice, our family at times became like 'a little bit of heaven on earth'.

"Children Arise" volumes 1 to 5, produced by my amazing sister Merrilyn Billing, and a tribute to her wonderful musical gift, were some of the fruit that came from those years when we as a family determined to not just learn Scriptures, but...**DO WHAT IT SAID!** We began an amazing journey, and the following pages tell the story of that journey.

I pray that this story may start you, the parent of those beautiful children that God has blessed you with, on your own adventure as a family, the exciting adventure of not only learning God's Word through music, but also learning to practice it, DO it, and learn how to make it work in your own life and the lives of those precious children. God once showed me a picture: every verse I taught the children was like giving them a most beautiful jewel, and it was a beautiful treasure for them to keep.

This is the story of our adventure as a family. May the following pages excite you to begin your own adventure! Yours will be different from ours but I know it will be just as exciting! Yes parents! Now is the time to **ARISE!**

Chapter 1:

PARENTS ARISE!

"And all thy children shall be taught of the Lord and great shall be the peace of thy children."

Isaiah 54:13 (KJV). Children Arise Vol.1

It was a year I will never forget. Paul and I had three children, Andrea seven years, Jonathan five years and Michelle was one year old. This was the year that Paul decided to do extra study. He was a Biochemist at the Launceston General Hospital, and he decided he would like to study for a Fellowship in this area to further his career. This meant a full year of study for him so that by the time he took his exam in Melbourne he would know everything there was to know at that time about Biochemistry.

Every evening after we put the children to bed, Paul would go off to his make-shift study in our bedroom and study for a few hours at our old desk. Meanwhile I would be sitting in the lounge room, feeling sorry for myself and quite lonely. One evening as I sat there I thought to myself, "Paul is studying, what can I do?" As I prayed about it a thought began to come to me, "Teach the children Scripture!" This thought persisted and I began to search for a pack of Scripture cards that a friend of ours, Vince Misdom, had memorised through his association with a group called the Navigators. As I looked at the cards in my hand I became quite excited and pictured teaching our children Scriptures in this way too.

As a child I too had learnt many Scripture verses in Sunday School. We had a godly man called Basil Young who encouraged us children to learn many verses and psalms, and had rewarded us with gifts like pens, booklets, cards and recognition. I recalled all the times I had stood out the front of the Sunday School quoting the latest verse, psalm, even the books of the Bible, and the excitement I felt as I received my reward.

As I gazed at the pack of Scripture cards I began to picture our own children having a huge repertoire, and I began to pray and ask God how I could do this. A thought came to me, "teach the verses in song." This thought was just like a light bulb going on in my mind, and I felt so excited I could hardly wait to begin! But what verse to teach? Then I remembered one of the first verses Basil Young had taught me years before, and I decided that this would be the verse I would begin with. It was 1 Corinthians 10.13. "*There hath no temptation taken you but such as is common to man, but God is faithful who will not suffer you to be tempted above that ye are able, but will with the temptation make a way to escape that ye may be able to bear it.*"

The next day at breakfast I said to Paul, "The children are going to learn this verse, and they will quote it to you by the end of the week." When I quoted the verse to Paul (there were fifty words in it!) he rolled his eyes and just said, "We'll see." That's all I needed. "Yes," I thought, "*We will see*!"

I began by writing out the verse on a small card and placing it above the sink in the kitchen where I could see it clearly. At the time I had been reading many books on faith, all of which explained that faith was simply asking God for what you needed and then thanking Him for the answer. So I did! I simply asked God for a tune for this verse and thanked Him for it. As I read the verse and thought about it a tune came to me, and I ran to the piano to see if it would fit the verse. Sure enough it did, and after playing it through a few times I felt confident to teach it. I also played the tune onto my tape recorder so I wouldn't forget it, and as the week progressed I was totally amazed at how easily the children learnt such a hard verse. Friday tea time arrived and I planted the children in front of Paul while I went to the piano to play. They proceeded to sing the fifty word verse to him while he sat with his mouth hanging open. I was so excited! I knew that if the children could learn a verse of that size so easily through music, they could learn any verse.

Soon afterwards I was invited by a friend to hear a visiting speaker who had a prophetic ministry, and who was speaking at a tiny church in Exeter. I decided to go.

That night, as the speaker concluded his message, he asked if anyone would like to come and receive a 'word from the Lord'. I and many others went forward. When the speaker came to me he asked if I had any children. I told him I had three. He looked intently at me and said, "I have a word for you, and it's found in *Isaiah 54.13.*" "*And all thy children shall be taught of the Lord and great shall be the peace of thy children.*"

My eyes immediately filled with tears, and I felt as though God had just spoken clearly to my heart. He had given me an amazing confirmation that I was stepping into the plan he had for our family. I suddenly knew that as I taught Scripture to our children it would be God who would really be teaching them and His reward would be great peace in our home as our children learned to do life 'God's way'.

We had begun a new adventure that was to take us through the children's formative years and well into their teens. This adventure would revolutionise not only their lives but those of Paul and I as well, for not only would our children ARISE and become full of God's Word and learn His ways, but we as parents would also ARISE and become full of His Words and learn His ways too!

Chapter 2:

'YES MUM' 'YES DAD!'

"Children obey your parents in the Lord for this is right. Honour thy father and thy mother, this is the first commandment with a promise, that it may be well with thee and thou mayest live long on the earth."

Ephesians: 6 verses 1,2,3 (KJV). Children Arise Volume I

"Oooooooh but... *Do I have to*?" *"No! I don't WANT to*!" I'm sure it wasn't just in our household that these words were so common, or should I say, this whingeing, whining and arguing. It was time to really get started on our new journey.

Imagine my delight when I discovered the above amazing verse in Ephesians 6.

I knew my first job was to ask God for a tune. I wrote the verse onto a small card and placed it on the window-sill above my kitchen sink so I could look at it as I worked. I began to thank God for His tune to this verse. It wasn't long before a bright little tune began to play over and over in my mind and I quickly played it through on the piano a few times to make sure I remembered it. Now it was time to write the verse out on a large piece of cardboard, and think of a story to tell the children. I used stories about children the same ages as ours and with similar life experiences so our children would relate to what they heard.

The first story was the beginning of many where I chose an example of a child with a negative attitude. The stories always had a happy ending because the children had been taught the verse we were now learning and decided they had better change their ways and live the way God said they should.

Such a simple little story had the attention of Andrea, Jonny and Michelle as they sat in the lounge room eating their afternoon tea on that Monday afternoon after school. I sat on the piano stool while I listened to their chatting about their day at school. After sharing their news and finishing off their ginger nut crunch bickies it was now time to begin our Verse Time.

"Children," I began, "I have a special story to tell you today about Christine and Jason." When I explained that Christine and Jason were the exact same ages as Andrea and Jonny, they immediately looked up at me with great interest.

My story continued. "Both Christine and Jason were very naughty children. When Mum asked them to make their beds and tidy up their rooms there was a chorus of "Oooh! Do I have to?" Poor Mum was so tired of listening to their complaining and arguing she decided it was easier to do the jobs herself. However, she was not happy with Christine and Jason, as they were very disobedient children."

"One day Christine invited her friend Emma to come and play after school. Emma was horrified by Christine's rudeness and disobedience to her mother. Emma, who loved Jesus, asked Christine and Jason if they would come to Sunday school with her the next Sunday."

"That Sunday, during the lesson, the Sunday school teacher just happened to be speaking about the verse, '*children obey your parents in the Lord for this is right*'…etc. She then taught it to the class as a song. Poor Christine felt very embarrassed and guilty and when the lesson was finished, she began to cry loudly. Emma took her to the teacher. "I'm nasty and horrible!" Christine wailed, "I'm not obedient at all!" Jason was trying hard not to cry, but he too looked very upset. The teacher suggested that Christine and Jason tell Jesus how sorry they were and ask his forgiveness. After a short prayer she then suggested they go home and tell their mother that they were very sorry for being so disobedient."

"She also suggested that Christine and Jason say "yes Mum" or "yes Dad" each time they were asked to do something. Then they would be learning to be obedient the way God wanted them to."

"Imagine Mum's surprise and delight when the children arrived home and she heard a chorus of "yes Mum" when she asked them both to help set the table for lunch. She was even more thrilled when Dad came home from work and asked Jason to tidy up their toys. "Yes Dad," they chorused."

"Mum and Dad looked at each other with big smiles on their faces. They were so happy to have obedient children!"

"All week Christine and Jason found they were singing their new song, and the words kept reminding them to be obedient because that was what God wanted. The more the children practised their new verse the nicer they became and Mum and Dad decided to take them to Sunday school each week so they could all learn more about God."

As I concluded the story I realised Andrea, Jonny and Michelle had been listening so intently they were obviously identifying with Christine and Jason and remembering the times they had argued and complained themselves.

It was now time to teach the verse as a song, and, as I played it through to them on the piano, I was thrilled to find they picked up the tune almost immediately and could probably have quoted it back to me by the conclusion of our first session.

For the next four afternoons our verse times consisted of various activities to reinforce the training in obedience 'God's way'. The format for teaching this verse became the format we used every week. It was as follows:

Tuesday: -singing the new verse.

-quiz on Monday's story.

Wednesday: -singing with percussion instruments

-dot to dot activity sheet for each child consisting of the verse written in dots and needing to be joined. Andrea, Jonny and Michelle's work was displayed on the fridge or a notice board for the week.

Thursday: -singing the new verse.

-activity sheet for each child with the verse written out in double lines. The verse was coloured in by each child and again displayed for the week in a prominent place. Stamps or stickers were given to encourage them.

Friday: -quiz given to see if children could:

a.) Remember the story.

b.) Quote the verse.

- Sing the new verse.

- Verse Time diary. New exercise books were given to the children and they wrote the verse out and drew their own picture. Each child was given a gold star to show that they now knew the verse as a song and were putting it into practice. (I wrote the verse out for Michelle who was too young to do it herself.)

It wasn't long before… "yes Mum!" or "yes Dad" became more common than arguing and it was an absolute delight to be visiting another family or to be in town and hear a little voice say "Yes Mum" in the cutest way when I gave an instruction. It didn't happen all the time – but when it did I felt it was a true reward for the time I was investing in the children's regular 'Verse Times'.

As these 'true to life' stories unfolded (most times I myself hardly knew what was going to happen next!) I would watch the expressions of surprise and shock on the faces of our children as they identified with the characters in the story who were so much like them.

What an exciting way to teach! For weeks to come, whenever the children began to argue or complain when asked to do something, they would be reminded of Christine and Jason. It was great to be able to show them that God wanted them to react the right way too, not just Mum and Dad.

The ongoing rewards even in just teaching this one verse were HUGE. Our children became known as obedient children, and there was so much more peace in our family! Truly the verse I had been given was beginning to come to pass.

"And all thy children shall be taught of the Lord and great shall be the peace of thy children." Isaiah.54.13

Chapter 3:

The Prayer Box

"What is faith? It is the confident assurance that something we want is going to happen. It is the certainty that what we hope for is waiting for us even though we cannot see it up ahead." Hebrews 11:1 (TLB) Children. Arise Volume 4

"And in that day ye shall ask me nothing. Verily, verily, I say unto you whatsoever ye shall ask the Father in My name, He will give it unto you." John 16:23 (KJV) Children Arise Vol.1

"Every good gift and every perfect gift is from above and cometh down from the Father." James 1:17 (KJV) Children Arise Vol 5

"Again I say unto you that if two of you shall agree upon earth as touching anything that they shall ask, it shall be done for them by my Father, which is in heaven." Matthew 18:19 (KJV) (unrecorded).

"Therefore I say unto you, what things so-ever ye desire, when ye pray, believe that ye receive them and ye shall have them." Mark 11:24 (KJV)

It was the year we were living in Hobart. Andrea was in Grade three, she was almost eight years old, Jonny was in Prep and had just turned six, and Michelle was two and a half.

Paul had been invited to take charge of a Pathology Laboratory, supposedly for three months. Little did we know that those three months would stretch to thirteen months and would provide some of the best family time we were to experience in all those 'growing up' years.

When Paul first agreed to take the job we had been learning the verse in Hebrews 11.1 (quoted above). Then the 'Prayer Box' idea happened. It came from one of the books I was reading at the time. (The children groaned every time I told them I was reading a new book! I was always looking for the next 'new idea'.) The idea was that a specific request was written out and dated on a nice sized card with a space beneath the request for the answer and the date the answer was received.

It seemed like the perfect way to apply the verse we were learning at the time.

Our first specific prayer request was written on a lovely bright yellow piece of cardboard with plenty of space for the answer.

We needed accommodation in Hobart for our family of five for three months, at least. Andrea was having piano lessons so we needed access to a piano. We also needed a furnished home as we couldn't buy furniture for just three months. Also, because we loved to entertain guests, it would have been great to have some extra room. We concluded our request by asking for new friends for our children. So the first prayer card was written out.

"Dear Heavenly Father, Could we please have a furnished house in Hobart, close to a school with access to a piano for piano lessons, and preferably with extra room for some guests. And P.S. Could our children please have some friends near by. In Jesus Name, Amen." We left a place to write down the answer and, on the first night at tea time we made our request as a family. We each agreed together, and prayed and asked God very specifically for everything we needed.

It would have been wonderful to be able to say the prayer was answered immediately, but the weeks went by and we came close to the date we were to move to Hobart and still no house to rent.

The Company had offered to pay for us to rent a house, but it seemed there was nothing available. Certainly there wasn't anyone who was willing to rent to a family of five for just three months. Paul made inquiries each week but with no success. However, an interesting thing was happening. The more we thanked God each night for the answer, the more convinced we all became that He was in control, and He had somewhere ideal for us to live. Hebrews 11.1 was becoming a reality. We all had the confident assurance that what we wanted WAS going to happen! We were certain that what we hoped for WAS waiting for us, even though we could not see it up ahead.

Each of us, the children included, were firm in our conviction that what we had asked for would happen.

Two weeks before we were due to move we still had nowhere to stay. Paul phoned his new workplace, and in the course of conversation he mentioned that we still didn't have accommodation.

One week later – only seven days before we were due to move - the answer came. The Company would now pay for motel accommodation for us, but only for three months. Praise God! Something was finally happening on our behalf.

A week later we arrived in Hobart and were shown to a very small motel room in a lovely suburb of Hobart. By now, we had grown so accustomed to thanking God for this prayer answer we were excited to see what would happen next.

Jonny, Andrea, Michelle and Janine enjoying our time in Hobart

We had only stayed in this tiny apartment for one week when the owner of the motel came to us with a special offer. He owned a large three bedroom house just down the road which he also rented out, and when he noticed our family with three children he decided we were the ones he would like to offer this house to for the same rent as the tiny apartment.

So within one week of arriving in Hobart we were shown this most beautiful house, fully furnished, with magnificent views out over Mount Wellington, with room to have guests to stay, a huge open plan lounge, dining room and kitchen and within walking distance to a lovely little local school. As an added treat we were informed by the motel manager that we would have a cleaning lady coming every Tuesday morning to do a thorough clean of the house. Plus, because we were in temporary accommodation, Paul was eligible for a weekly food allowance which would enable us to be extremely hospitable in the coming months, and have many guests to stay. And as for the piano, we were almost inundated! The guy in the flat below was a professional pianist, so beautiful jazz music was playing most days. The local headmaster of the little school nearby offered to let us use the school piano any time after school hours for practice purposes, and upon visiting a magnificent home next door to us, owned by the Salvation Army as a retreat for unwed mothers, we were told we were most welcome to come in and use their piano at any time! Even the P.S. on our request was answered as we discovered there was a lovely American family living next door with two little girls near the ages of our children. Wow! As a family we were thanking God for His kindness.

This wonderful gift of accommodation for our family continued for the full thirteen months we stayed in Hobart.

During that year, as many family members and other friends came to stay with us, they too participated in our Bible readings and family prayer times around the dinner table in the evenings. We encouraged them to tell us of their own personal prayer requests and these were faithfully recorded and dated on our prayer cards and placed in our new 'Prayer Request Box'. To this day I still have the prayer cards we wrote during that thirteen months, and, when we finally moved back to Launceston at the end of that time I counted eighty four cards with answers that had been received by our family. Some of those answers were a "Yes!" some were a "No." Some were answers to tiny requests, and some were answers to huge requests and were the most amazing miracles.

Our adventure was continuing. As a family we were now learning a new way, telling God about our needs and leaving them with Him. We were learning as a group to thank Him while we waited, and the request sitting in the box reminded us that we were learning to exercise our faith and trust in our loving Heavenly Father. Hebrews 11.1 was becoming more of a reality to all of us.

When Paul and I discovered the books by E.W. Kenyon and Kenneth Hagin, known to many as Fathers of Faith we read every one we could find. It was so exciting to find people who were so far ahead of us in this journey of trusting and believing what God said, and applying His Words to daily life.

We were also learning an important lesson. We couldn't manipulate God to answer "Yes" every time. Sometimes the answer was "No," but *always* there was an answer and as we observed the miracles of answered prayer occurring we realized that, *"Every good gift and every perfect gift is from above and cometh down from the Father" James 1.17 Vol 5.* A tune to this verse was born as a thank you to God for His goodness. *(Children Arise Vol 5.)*

From Parent to Parent.

The Prayer Box continued throughout the years our children were at home and it was a huge help in teaching them *not to worry – but to pray!* Later, during their teen years there were many of their friends who were encouraged to place their request in our Prayer Box and to wait and trust for their answer to come. There were requests for jobs, future husbands and wives…but that's another story.

Prayer request. Date:

Answer to request. Date:

Chapter 4:

I'M SORRY! THAT'S ALRIGHT.

"And be ye kind one unto another, tender hearted, forgiving one another, even as God for Christ's sake has forgiven you." Ephesians, 4:32 (KJV). Children Arise Vol.2

"A good marriage consists of two good forgivers."

I had just finished reading a book by Bob Barnes about marriage, and this quote really stood out to me.

Our family was back home after our year away, and we were on our Christmas break at our shack at Low Head. I was wading through my usual pile of books on raising children and on having a good marriage. Each year in January it was my re-evaluation time. How was I doing as a wife? Could I learn something more to improve our marriage? Was there something more I could learn to improve the life of our family? Was there something new to teach the children? This particular day I sat relaxing on a banana lounge taking notes from books and planning which ideas I would begin to implement through the coming year in the life of our family.

Every time I announced at the tea table "Guess what, I have a new idea!" There would be a chorus of groans. "Oh No!" "Not another one!" However, right now I was having a ball, doing what I liked doing best, relaxing with a new teaching book, eating chocolate and taking notes as I made a new plan. As I mulled over the quote I had just read, I wondered, "Does that mean a good family consists of five or six good forgivers?" I was about to find out. I thought back to the time when I was first married. The words "I'm sorry" were not in my vocabulary – neither were the words "I forgive you." I was amazed to hear Paul say them so easily. I could not acknowledge my own mistakes and weaknesses, nor could I easily release others from my judgements upon them – particularly if I thought they had done something 'unfair' or 'unjust'.

As I had been teaching our children Scriptures to music I realized I too needed to change. How could I encourage them to say they were sorry when they spoke abruptly or in nasty tones to their friends and to each other if I couldn't do that myself. I recognised there were some hard walls of pride in my own life.

A new journey had begun for us as a family as we were learning to apply these Scriptures we were singing daily. It was a journey where Paul and I would be learning and changing along with our children. Particularly me, as I needed the biggest overhaul! Paul has always had, and still has, the kindest, nicest temperament, and I have always been so blessed to have such a calm, peaceable, loving husband and father to our children. For his wife to still say that after thirty six years of marriage, he has to be VERY special!

So, this summer, we as a family learnt to sing this verse.

"And be ye kind one unto another, tender hearted, forgiving one another, even as God for Christ's sake has forgiven you." Ephesians 4.32

Changes began to happen as we began to apply this verse practically into our family life. We each began to look for ways to be kind to each other and little bunches of flowers began to arrive in the house, picked by the children for Mum. As we continued to sing the words and talk about them every day we discussed the best way to forgive each other, and we came up with a very practical application of the words, *"tender hearted, forgiving one another."*

"I'm sorry Andrea!" said Jonny, as he put his eight year old arms around his tall sister. Jonny had a wicked grin on his face. He loved teasing the girls. "That's alright." mumbled Andrea, standing stiffly. "Give him a hug Andrea," Paul encouraged, so stiff arms went around Jonny, and she softened once again towards this cute but irritating brother of hers.

We suddenly had children who were hugging each other regularly! Paul and I began to insist on a new pattern of behaviour within the family. The words, "I'm sorry!" and, "that's alright" accompanied by a hug were becoming an everyday occurrence. Although some of the hugs were rather stiff, it helped the wronged child to recover quickly. But how could I, as their mother, encourage this continual behaviour of kindness and forgiveness without practicing it too?

So began a change in Janine Targett as I found myself regularly asking for forgiveness too, and being granted it (which was lovely). Both Andrea and Jonny told me at different times, "Mum, You can't KEEP asking for forgiveness!" This Scripture was helping to knock down my wall of pride, and it was such a relief to be able to admit it when I made a mistake or lost my temper. I was experiencing the benefits of teaching the children to do life God's Way.

The Targett family had now become a family of huggers! Even Andrea, who was not naturally a hugger (like her mother), was encouraged to get her arms right around her brother or sister and forgive and hug.

Forgiving and hugging became so commonplace in our family life that even through the teenage years, our children would drape themselves over Paul and I even when we were at Church and other public places. It was so much a part of our lives to show affection that I watched a miracle take place of love and care for each other. Today, as young adults, they each continue to hug each other and Paul and I. Now, our wonderful new extended family of in-laws, Lynden, Verity and Joe and our thirteen grandchildren are also inundated with hugs and a warm feeling of belonging in our growing clan.

That freedom of caring for others and forgiving with a hug, was now outreaching into the lives of those around us. I hoped people didn't want to run the other way when they saw one of us coming because - watch out! They would probably receive a huge hug.

"And be ye kind one unto another, tender-hearted, forgiving one another, even as God for Christ's sake has forgiven you." Ephesians, 4.32

Chapter 5:

The Class Bully

"But I say unto you that hear, love your enemies, do good to them that hate you, bless them that curse you, and pray for them that despitefully use you." Luke 6:27,28 (KJV). Children Arise. Vol.3.

Nadine was the class bully. A tall girl, much taller than the other girls, she was beautiful looking, but with a character that didn't match her outward appearance. She had a following of girls who almost worshipped the ground she walked on. To get her approval they would do whatever she said to do.

Nadine loved the power she had over the other girls, and if they became a part of her 'in group' they were popular, but if not, they were bullied by 'the gang.'

Andrea was very much her own person – she was never interested in following a crowd, so this year, in Grade five, at ten years of age she was quite happy with her own couple of friends. Andrea was one who really didn't care what anyone else thought about her…until now.

I could tell there was something wrong when we had our usual 'Verse Time' that afternoon. I sensed Andrea's thoughts were elsewhere. She looked so unhappy and I knew she wasn't going to tell us as a group what was bothering her. I made a mental note to have a chat later, when she was in bed.

When each of our children went to bed at night Paul and I had begun (or been conned into, I'm not sure which) a routine where one or the other of us would go and have a quiet chat and a pray with them before they went off to sleep. Michelle had already decided that if she prayed with us each night that she would have 'nice luscious dreams', and sleep without nightmares. Therefore she would call us in to pray with her in case we were too busy and forgot. So began a night-time ritual with the three which continued for years. A chat, a prayer and a hug, then "Good night. Love you!"

Looking back later I realised that, with Andrea's nature, had she not had those opportunities each night to be listened to just by herself, her life would have been a closed book and I may never have had the chance to understand her need for quality time and individual attention. She found it difficult to share her thoughts with more than one person at a time and, if we had not provided this opportunity each night – in a busy household I would never have discovered the quiet inner strength and wise thoughts that this daughter of ours had.

I knew it would be really important to talk to Andrea that night, and, sure enough, when it was her turn for some individual attention the story poured from her with sobs and tears.

Nadine had taken a dislike to Andrea, and had been encouraging her little gang to bully her. Nadine herself, the chief bully, was really giving Andrea a hard time. The more she talked and cried I could see that Andrea had had a terrible day with Nadine pushing and shoving and throwing nasty taunts. Andrea had no idea how to handle all this negative attention she was receiving. She felt ill and didn't want to go to school the next day.

My natural reaction as her mother was to march straight up to school the next morning and speak to this bully myself. Give her a piece of my mind. Protect my daughter!

Years before, my own mother had done exactly that when, in a similar position to Andrea, I had experienced daily verbal bullying from two 'friends'. My mother had finally had enough of me coming home from school feeling ill every night and she had arrived at the High School one day and told the girls to stop bullying her daughter. The girls had gleefully continued, knowing they had really upset me, something a true bully totally enjoys doing. So, while my first inclination was to follow in Mum's footsteps and protect my girl, we had just been learning an exciting new verse in song and this just looked like the perfect opportunity to react God's way.

I asked Andrea, "What does that verse say that we're learning at the moment?" In a quavering voice she quoted it, *"But I say unto you that hear, love your enemies, do good to those who hate you, bless them that curse you and pray for them that despitefully use you!"* Paul had now joined us, and we all agreed that Nadine was certainly an enemy at the moment, so we began by asking Andrea to pray and forgive Nadine. The verse suggested we pray for her and bless her, so we all did that together. As Andrea forgave and asked God to bless and help Nadine to change and become a nicer girl, the tears dried up and a little smile appeared.

When she arrived home from school the next day I was waiting for her news. "How was the day? How did Nadine treat you?" Andrea was not really one to share too much when her brother and sister were around. She usually wanted some quiet time to herself when she arrived home from a day with lots of people, so I had to be patient and wait until she was in bed that night. Her report was amazing, and so encouraging. For the first time in weeks Nadine did not say anything nasty to her at all. Andrea was so surprised! She nervously waited all day for the usual bullying but absolutely nothing happened.

That evening, again, Andrea prayed and spoke out forgiveness and again asked God to bless Nadine and the other bullies. As we continued this pattern, her reports became better with each passing day. Not only was Nadine no longer bullying Andrea physically and verbally, now she was also telling her friends to stop as well! Andrea's amazement grew as we continued to encourage her to react God's way.

It was not long before Nadine was beginning to change quite dramatically. The bullying stopped completely, and she began to become quite protective of Andrea. If she saw any of her friends treating Andrea the way they used to she would stop them immediately! The reports we were receiving each day continued to amaze us all.

One day Andrea received an invitation to Nadine's birthday party, and when she went and actually enjoyed herself we knew a miracle had taken place.

The time came when Andrea wanted to invite Nadine to our home and we finally met this girl who had been the class bully, and who was now one of Andrea's best friends.

As our family gave her friendship and hospitality, I knew that I could never have done that, if I too, as Andrea's mother, had not been practicing this verse on her behalf. My natural reaction in the past would have been, "No Way! Nadine can't come HERE to play with you Andrea! Not when she's treated YOU the way SHE has!"

God had changed me as well. I was able to accept Andrea's new friendship with Nadine, and be glad that God had so dramatically changed 'the class bully' when Andrea had agreed to react God's way.

From Parent to Parent.

This lesson has never been forgotten by our children. Over the next few years there were many times when opportunities brought a choice – would they react their way or God's way to others who mistreated them?

Paul and I have observed that they have each grown into much healthier, happier young adults (both emotionally and physically) for learning to do life 'God's way'.

Last Sunday at church, a young parent, Isaac, tapped me on the shoulder and said his daughter wanted to sing something to me. As I knelt down to look into the eyes of his three year old daughter, Naomi, she began to sing so sweetly,

"Do not merely listen to the Word and so deceive yourselves, do what it says," James 1.22 (NIV) Children Arise Volume 4

Confirmation? Thank you God. I hear you!

Chapter 6:

Freedom for the Fearful Child

"For God Has not given us a spirit of fear but of love and of power and of a sound mind."
2 Timothy 1:7 (KJV) Children Arise Volume 2.

Jonny was our fearful child. Even as a baby he was frightened. He would stiffen and cry loudly if I turned on the vacuum cleaner, or if there was any other unexpected noise. It was as though he was born with a certain amount of stress, and certainly, as I looked back I realized my pregnancy with him had been stressful.

During the nine months I carried him I had taught music at a local Primary school, and on the day he was due to be born I was conducting the school choir at a special Christmas concert for the school. Back then Andrea was just a toddler, and she came to school each day while I taught, and we had moved house when I was seven months pregnant. I had also insisted on doing a course in design and dressmaking that year, and the exam was extremely stressful, as I was totally determined that I had to pass it. The exam was held the same week we moved house. I was involved in a singing group at the same time called 'The Cousins', and practice was in our home on Monday evenings. We produced our second record while I was pregnant with Jonny, and weekends found us singing at numerous venues around Tasmania. All in all it was a very busy pregnancy!

I have since noticed that those women who have relatively stress free pregnancies also seem to give birth to happy, stress free babies. Poor Jonny was not off to a good start! I began to notice something else too. Because I had quite an outgoing personality and could become quite bossy, if I spoke to Jonny too loudly and became angry with him, he would begin to cough within the hour and become ill with a cough or cold for the next few days. Certainly Jonny's stress levels were high, and he could not take confrontation without it affecting him physically.

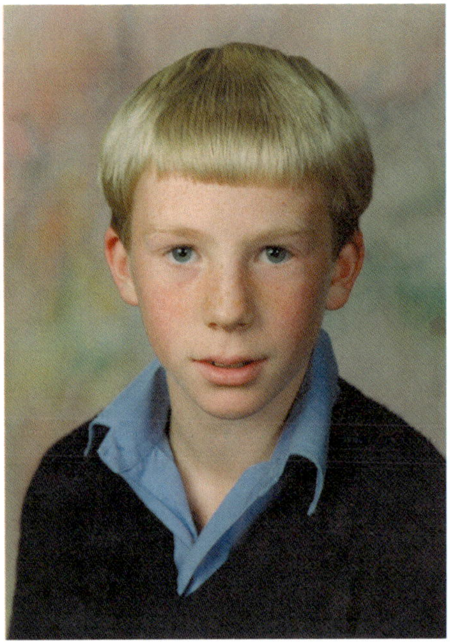

A timid Jonny at Primary School

Having since read the book 'Personality Plus' by Florence Littauer, I realised Jonny was a phlegmatic, sanguine temperament and he didn't like any kind of confrontation. His temperament loved peace and fun, and preferably no stress! Unfortunately however life does bring stress to us, and the results of this showed in the many coughs and colds and sicknesses Jonny had as a small boy. He was a delightful child, with white blond hair, huge almond shaped blue eyes and a gorgeous cheeky grin that showed us he couldn't wait to grow up enough to begin playing practical jokes by teasing his sisters, which he did mercilessly through the years.

When Jonny finished his last year at Primary School and moved on to High School it was the most stressful year of his life. Along with all the other children his age, he moved out of the safe environment of a single classroom and one teacher, to a huge school where he had to move to different classes with different teachers throughout the day. A pattern began to emerge. Jonny would come out for breakfast on a Thursday morning and he would either feel sick or have a pain in his tummy. When he came home from school on a Thursday he usually had a headache. As the weeks went by, Jonny was averaging one Thursday a fortnight where he would stay home because of the bad tummy pains he had in the morning.

Paul and I decided we had better have him checked, so we took him to the doctor. After a thorough consultation the doctor called us in for a private chat, and asked us what was causing stress in Jonny's life. He said he thought he was a candidate for an ulcer, and that the problems all appeared to be stress related! Paul and I were quite stunned. Our boy with an ulcer at the age of eleven? If it hadn't already happened, then we certainly didn't want it to happen.

When we arrived home we sat with Jonny and had a serious discussion. What was happening on a Thursday that was upsetting him? The more Jonny shared, the picture became clearer. The teacher in charge of Jonny's home class was an extremely loud, domineering man, and he also taught Jonny for Social Science on a Thursday. As Jonny was not familiar with the school he had been late to one of his Social Science classes and was reprimanded in front of the whole class. As a result he was terrified to go to his Thursday class in case the same thing happened again, hence the pains and headaches.

He was also fearful of the big Grade ten boys, particularly a group of bullies who watched out for the small Grade seven boys at lunch times and who teased and made fun of them. Some of these boys were also on his school bus and Jonny had not yet developed the confidence and social skills to be able to cope with them.

We couldn't just remove Jonny from the school as he would have encountered these problems anyway at another place or time. We realised we needed God's help and wisdom. Paul and I began to pray. As I was now regularly teaching Scripture to the children through music I began to ask God for a verse that might help Jonny. As I was doing my housework one day another light bulb moment suddenly occurred. I remembered a verse I had learnt years before as a teenager, when, like Jonny, I was also full of fears.

The verse was, *2 Timothy 1.7 "For God has not given us the spirit of fear, but of love, and of power and of a sound mind."*

I was instantly full of faith. I knew that this verse had the power to set Jonny completely free! The memories from years before raced through my mind as I ran down the passage of our home calling loudly for Jonny. I remembered how, as a teenager working in a local bookshop in my spare time, I had become frozen with fear as I became aware that customers might be looking at my hands as I wrapped their parcels or wrote out their dockets. The more self conscious I had become the more it began to affect me, until my hands would shake, my mouth would go dry and my heart would begin to race. At the time I had searched that bookshop for a book about nerves, and, when finding one on the subject, I read it and received absolutely no help whatsoever. As my fears worsened I became terrified of eating in front of others as my fork would shake all the way from my plate to my mouth. I remembered the awful feeling of dread when I was first invited to Paul's home for a meal before we were married. When my future Mum-in-law asked me a question I was unable to lift the fork from the plate, I was so self-conscious and filled with terror. When I finally managed the feat my hand shook compulsively, and looked so ridiculous that I thought at the time I would never be able to do anything in front of people again.

All these thoughts raced through my mind as I called out to Jonny, anxious to give him the answer to his problem. I remembered how, when I first heard this verse I had quoted it daily as though it were my lifeline, and it had become that as it set me free from the paralysing effects of fear as a teenager.

"Jonny," I shouted. "This is your verse! This is for you!" I sat with him and proceeded to tell him my own story, and how this verse had set me free years before. I encouraged him to begin to speak it out each day when he first stepped onto the school bus, and when he arrived at school and had to walk to different classrooms. I especially encouraged him to speak his verse whenever he was going into a stressful situation such as his Social Science class, or at lunchtime when the big bullies were around.

Over the next few days I put this verse to music and we began to sing it as a family. We sang it daily when the children arrived home from school. I would make sure they all had something to eat, then we would sit around in the lounge room and talk about the day. Before long I would be playing the tune on the piano and the children would sing the verse while we thought about what it meant to us.

Over the next few weeks I would ask Jonny if he was remembering to quote his special verse and he would nod his head and grin at me. The day came when we were travelling to a nearby town as a family. Suddenly, from the back seat, Jonny's voice piped up, "Mum?"

"Yes Jon."

"Mum, you know that verse you made me say all the time? About not having a spirit of fear but of power, love and a sound mind?"

"Yes, Jon."

"Well, it works!" said Jonny.

Paul and I looked around at him with surprise.

"Yes," he said. "I kept saying it all the time and now I'm not afraid anymore!"

Wow! What a great moment for Paul and I. We looked at each other with a big smile and asked him to tell us more. Sure enough, it appeared that God had set him completely free from all fear. In fact, over the next few weeks, months, and later, years, Jonny changed so dramatically that my sister Mandie said she had never seen such a complete change in a child ever before.

Jonny changed from a boy who was timid, nervy, and shy to a funny, entertaining leader amongst his friends. He confidently wore all sorts of outrageous outfits, funny hats and crazy shirts. As he grew older he was free to compose his own loud, teenage tunes to many of the verses he had previously learnt to much milder tunes. He formed a band called Grrrr, and became the lead singer. He bravely shouted the songs he wrote at the top of his voice whilst playing his guitar. He grew his hair long and attracted his own following of young teenagers who wanted to be 'just like Jonny T'.

God set Jonny free from many other fears at the same time as he meditated on, sang and quoted his special verse.

Another big fear was the fear of water. Up to this point Jonny had not even been able to get his head under water during swimming lessons, as he was so terrified of water. During this time of being set free from fears, Jonny found he could now swim, dive, and now water sports became his favourite past-time. He became an avid surfer and swimmer, and when he first drove a car it could be seen travelling off to the beach with a car load of mates and a few surf boards on the roof.

There is a verse that says *"whom the Son sets free shall be free indeed"*, and Jonny had certainly been set free.

Jonny and Michelle. The beginning of a fearless surfer

Jonny graduating from UTAS

Jonny is now married to Verity, and has two young boys, Sonny and Kipp. He has completed five years of University study, gaining two degrees and has trained to become an English, Social - Science Teacher!

When I think back to those days when Jonny was so frightened of his English, Social- Science teacher I would never, ever have believed it possible that he would become a teacher himself. He is now a very popular teacher, still with a huge love of music and a composer in his own right. He loves people! He loves life! He loves water and he especially loves Verity and his cute boys.

God has set him free!

Chapter 7:

THE PILOT STRIKE

"What is faith, it is the confident assurance that something we want is going to happen. It is the certainty that what we hope for is waiting for us even though we cannot see it up ahead." Hebrews 11:1 (TLB) Children Arise Vol 4.

"Don't worry about anything, instead pray about everything. Tell God your needs and don't forget to thank Him for the answers. If you do this you will experience God's peace, which is far more wonderful than the human mind can understand, His peace will keep your thoughts and hearts quiet and at rest as you trust in Christ Jesus." Philippians 4:6 –7 (TLB) Children Arise Vol.1

"But if you stay in me and obey my commands you may ask any request you like and it will be granted." John 15:7 (KJV) (unrecorded)

"And in that day ye shall ask me nothing, verily, verily I say unto you, whatsoever ye shall ask the Father in my Name, He will give it unto you." John 16:23(KJV) Children Arise Vol1

It was the now famous National pilot strike in Australia. It was also the month my sister Merrilyn Billing was recording Children Arise volume 2 in Brisbane.

As planes ground to a halt across the nation and panicked holiday makers cancelled their trips away, the Targett family continued their preparations to fly from Tasmania to Brisbane. Andrea, Jonathan and Michelle were to take part in the recording while Paul and I would be available to provide meals and generally be a support to the Billing family in any way we could. Michelle was seven, Jonathan was eleven and Andrea almost thirteen. The children had learnt the verse in Hebrews 11.1 (quoted above) and they were about to have an opportunity to put it into practice, not once, but many times throughout the next month!

Even though our fares had been paid, most flights were no longer even available and many holiday makers were cashing in their tickets and getting their money back. As a family we believed God wanted us in Brisbane, so when asked by friends if we were cancelling we told them we were still going! We believed as we prayed together as a family that we were meant to go, and we based our decision on our trust in God and His promise in Hebrews 11 verse 1. We were about to embark on one of the biggest adventures of our lives. We began to thank God that we would arrive in Brisbane, and the children would sing on Volume 2.

The day we were due to travel was a typical day during the strike. No-one really knew what type of plane - if any - they would be able to travel in, and there was no guarantee that we would be able to fly the three legs of the journey, as the situation was different in every airport. We had been informed by the airport officials that we would link up with another plane to Sydney when we arrived in Melbourne. There would be three legs to this journey: Launceston to Melbourne; Melbourne to Sydney; Sydney to Brisbane; then the Billings and the Children Arise Volume 2 recording!

As most domestic planes were grounded, Hercules army planes and large Jumbo jets from Malaysia had been enlisted to fly in and help with the crisis.

Paul decided to drive out to the airport ahead of time that morning to make sure we could travel. When he arrived back he was suddenly full of doubts, wondering what he was doing, taking his family of five on such a trip. He had just been charged an extra $850 on top of the fares we had paid, and this took most of the spending money for our trip. He had also discovered the only plane was an Australian air-force one travelling to Melbourne, and it would be a very noisy, rough ride.

By now, as a family, we were committed to going, so we formed the first of many prayer huddles and asked God to please return our $850 when we arrived in Brisbane, (or we would have no money to spend!) and for God to get us there safely. Paul had been told by the fellow who charged him the extra money that he could probably get it back if he called into the Qantas office in Brisbane and explained the situation when he arrived.

We were trusting God for our first miracle on this adventure.

As our children excitedly boarded the strange looking green and black air-force plane with Paul and I an hour later, they were filled with excitement. What an adventure!

We were all strapped securely into large, rather uncomfortable bare steel seats facing each other. The interior of the plane was a huge unlined cavity unlike anything we had ever seen before. It took off with a loud roar and we were on our way on one of the most exciting adventures in the life of our family.

Upon arrival at the airport in Melbourne we were informed there would be no planes at all travelling to Sydney until the next day - we were now stranded. After another prayer huddle with the children asking God for help, Paul placed a call to some of our relatives in Melbourne, and before long we were on our way out to their home on one of the many quaint trams that wound throughout the city and suburbs of Melbourne.

When the five of us arrived on the doorstep of my Aunt and Uncle's home it must have been a huge shock to my shy, retiring relatives who rarely had any visitors call – let alone a family of five with their large cases, looking for a bed for the night. With true Austin hospitality they rallied to help us and we spent a few memorable hours with Darrell and Doreen Austin and their children.

To this day I am amazed that my Aunt Doreen remained so calm and coped so well – even taking a photo of us all as we stood waiting for the taxi to take us back to the airport to catch our plane to Sydney the next morning.

At the Melbourne airport we were informed we would be travelling on a Jumbo Jet which had been flown in from Singapore to help with the crisis. Three little sets of eyes nearly popped out of their heads as the children gazed out the window in the waiting area and caught sight of the massive plane they were about to travel on. Wow! It was huge! This plane took off with an even louder roar than the air-force plane. It was so wide there appeared to be at least ten seats across, and our excitement mounted as we headed closer to our destination. We hit the tarmac in Sydney with a huge roar of engines. We had arrived on the second leg of our trip!

Once again we were informed to our dismay that there were no connecting flights to Brisbane that day and we would have to come back the next morning to possibly catch another Jumbo Jet *if* it came in from Singapore overnight. There would be no guarantees, but if we could be back at the airport at 9.00 next morning they would try to help us get to Brisbane.

By this time we were all tired from the excitement of the trip, and it was almost evening. Paul waited in a long line for quite some time, only to be told that all accommodation was completely booked out at the surrounding hotels and they couldn't help us unless we wanted to catch a taxi into the city and stay at a hotel an hour or so away. We would have to cover all the costs, and we wondered if we would have to spend the night sitting in the airport. Surely God had a better plan than that for us? For the third time in two days we grouped together while Paul prayed and asked God to show us what to do next. He asked God to please provide a bed somewhere for us all for the night.

Half an hour later Paul remembered a good friend he had made a few years before when he had worked in Sydney before we were married. After phoning his mate he was told his wife would be out to pick us all up within thirty minutes.

Wow! His wife was so kind, she was like an angel! Jill arrived with a huge smile and informed us that her parents were away for two weeks and she was looking after their home while they were away. She said she *knew* they wouldn't mind if we all stayed the night, and, within half an hour we were pulling up outside a beautiful home on one of the waterways of Sylvania Waters in Sydney.

Once again our children were amazed and excited when they found this beautiful home had a swimming pool. It was like a tropical paradise! Paul and I were given a spacious room with en-suite and the children had their own rooms. Our guardian angel, Jill, left us with a little box of food for tea and breakfast next day, and smiled and waved as she drove away.

I was more grateful than anyone else that night as we slept in our luxurious surroundings and thanked God as a little family for His kindness to us in providing this lovely place to stay.

When Jill arrived the next morning to take us back to the airport we were all so grateful! It had been quite an adventure, and now the children were seeing the suburbs of Sydney as we went on our sightseeing tour back to the airport.

While Jill waited with us to make sure we caught a plane to Brisbane she chatted to me and began to share about a huge crisis which was occurring in her marriage at that time. As I offered to pray for her, she smiled and hugged me through her tears and said God must have sent me to her! I thought God had sent her to us, but whichever way it was we were all very grateful and blessed to have met for that short time. To Paul and myself, it was an encouragement that God had worked out everything for good, and it was a great lesson for our children that God had sorted our problems out for us when we had prayed and asked Him.

As we took off in the next huge Jumbo Jet our faith in God to get us all to Brisbane was now being rewarded. We were on the final leg of our journey, and we would soon be meeting my sister Merrilyn, and her husband Graeme, and their two children Carolyn and Christopher. What excitement when we touched down on the tarmac of Brisbane airport – again with a loud roar of engines from the huge Jumbo Jet we were travelling in. By now our children were so excited they could hardly wait to see their cousins!

The Targett family in Brisbane at last!

We had arrived at our destination in the middle of our country's one and only National Pilot strike. Two days later, our full $850 was returned in cash after yet another prayer huddle and request from our family for a miracle We were full of faith and excitement as we began the second part of this amazing adventure.

"What is faith? It is the confident assurance that something we want is going to happen, it is the certainty that what we hope for is waiting for us even though we cannot see it up ahead." Hebrews 11.1 Children Arise volume 4.

Plane to Melbourne.

Accommodation.

Plane to Sydney.

Accommodation.

Plane to Brisbane.

Money back.

Thank you Lord!

Chapter 8:

The Recording

"Don't worry about anything; instead, pray about everything; Tell God your needs and don't forget to thank Him for the answers. If you do this you will experience God's peace, which is far more wonderful than the human mind can understand. His peace will keep your thoughts and your hearts quiet and at rest as you trust in Christ Jesus." Philippians 4.6 -7 (TLB) Children Arise Vol 1.

"The Lord will rescue me from every evil attack and bring me safely to His heavenly kingdom. To Him be glory for ever and ever, Amen." 2 Timothy 4.18 (NIV) Children Arise Vol.1

"The Lord detests lying lips but He delights in men who are truthful." Proverbs 12. 22. (NIV) Children Arise Vol 2

As we arrived at the Billing's home my mind flashed back to the time my sister Merry had come to visit us in Tasmania. As she listened to our children having 'Verse Time' around the piano one afternoon God had given her inspiration.

"Neen," she had exclaimed, "Other parents need to hear these songs and teach their children. Can I take your songs with me and record them in Brisbane?" Now, here we were, becoming involved with the recording process. How exciting!

Being in Brisbane for the recording of Children Arise Volume 2 was such a privilege, but it was also a lot of hard work.

Paul and I were there to keep the household running smoothly for the next three weeks, so, for us it would be a working holiday. Our job was to provide all meals for the Billing family and keep the home running smoothly. This would free them to work with the group of children Merry had been training. We would be available to pray and cook and help where ever we were required.

Meanwhile, Andrea, Jonny and Michelle had the excitement of joining the group that was being trained to sing all the Scriptures Merry had chosen for this Volume.

As with all the Children Arise recordings, we encountered opposition in many forms. I knew God was showing me that we needed prayer support for this project, and Merry suggested that the mothers of the singers might like to become the prayer support group.

From that time on, the parents would arrive with their children for practices, and we would pray in one room while the children sang in another. I remembered again how difficult it had been to even get the songs up to the Billings in the first place. My sister Mandie and I had encountered so many problems, and had used four tape recorders altogether as each one had either stopped working or distorted the music we were trying to record.

This recording was not going to be completed without a huge amount of prayer. As we met regularly and prayed for every stage of the recording and for the many problems along the way, I realized again how important it had been for our family to arrive in Brisbane as both a practical and a prayer support to the Billing family.

For Andrea, Jonathan and Michelle the next two weeks were a time of fun, excitement and hard work.

Firstly the children were all taken to a local clothes outlet and outfitted in pink, green or yellow shorts and T-shirts with coloured braces to match. They looked great! Then there were photos to be taken for the cover of the CD.

The only time I, as their mum, felt very flat was the afternoon Paul and I were busy cooking a meal. Everyone raced off to meet at a park for photos, and, because we were in the kitchen cooking, we had no idea where to go to watch the session. When the door slammed shut with the last of the children and parents racing off for photos and the house went quiet I looked at Paul in dismay and promptly burst into tears. We had just missed out on watching the excited children posing for their photos in their cute outfits, and we had no idea where they had gone!

I guess every exciting adventure has to have a low point, and I had reached mine. Not being a real servant at heart (unlike my wonderful husband) I had found it incredibly hard to be away from the practice room along with the other mothers while we got on with the job of praying for the success of the recording. And now being stuck in the kitchen, through my own choice, and missing out on the photos, it was all too much for my sanguine, fun nature to bear. I was ready to go home.

Photo shoot for Children Arise Volume 2

Paul did what he always did well, made me a cup of tea and prayed for me. It was my turn for some prayer and care. This 'servant business' was not my thing I decided, so Paul, in his quiet, gentle, kind way, decided I should go with the group the next day to the recording studio and be a part of the excitement. He would stay at home and have a meal ready for us all when we arrived back home in the evening. He also reminded me of the verse I had taught our children in Philippians 4.4-7, our family's antidote to worry. He suggested firmly and kindly, as only Paul can, that I pray and turn all my worries over to God, and begin to thank Him for the answers.

After a cuppa, a prayer and some quality time with Paul, my best mate, I was once again ready for whatever the next two weeks would hold.

Paul kept his word, and faithfully provided meals and a peaceful haven to come home to over the next two weeks while the hectic round of recording began.

There was a special Chinese Dragon festival happening in the streets below the recording studio that week, and from the first day Merry and the children were in the studio they began complaining of headaches, lethargy and other ailments. The mothers prayed for each child, as, one by one, they would be sent out to the little staff-room where we provided drinks and food.

Our prayer group of mums began to work overtime (goodness knows what the sound engineer thought!) We prayed for freedom in that room from the presence of evil, and for protection of every person involved in the recording.

We were not to know back then just HOW important it was to have these verses recorded for others to hear, sing and put into practice. Many found their lives radically changed by God as a result. Later, stories would come from other countries around the world telling of miracles and blessing as the CD was placed in people's hands and they began to sing God's powerful Words.

Certainly on this particular day, it was like all hell breaking loose to stop the recording, and I finally felt I was in my correct niche for the job – interceding. Each day was very hard work for Merry and the children. There were long hours of going over and over songs, and so many times the recording equipment would stop working. Sound engineers would be scratching their heads and saying things like "I don't understand. This has never happened before!" In fact this has been the refrain from sound engineers with the recording of all five volumes so far!

During this time of recording Michelle was able to sing a solo. Her voice sounded so cute with her lisp because of her missing two front teeth.

"The Lord detests lying lips but He delights in men who are truthful." Proverbs 12.22

For our three children, being part of the recording process was an amazing experience, especially as they had been singing these simple verses and others like them in their own lounge room back home for the last six years on an almost daily basis.

To hear some of those same songs being sung with the beautiful backing tracks my sister Merry had helped produce was an amazing treat for them, and even more so for their mother who had only played basic piano accompaniment back home. Merry had been gifted in an amazing way to be able to picture so many beautiful instruments accompanying these songs. (At this time of writing she has just completed Children Arise Volume 5 and 'the songs' are now going out to the next generation!)

Every evening we would bring the recorded music back home and play it during dinner. As we listened to it, both Paul and I felt rewarded for trusting God to get our family to Brisbane to be a part of this wonderful, exciting and sometimes difficult experience.

Merrilyn Billing conducting children at the recording studio

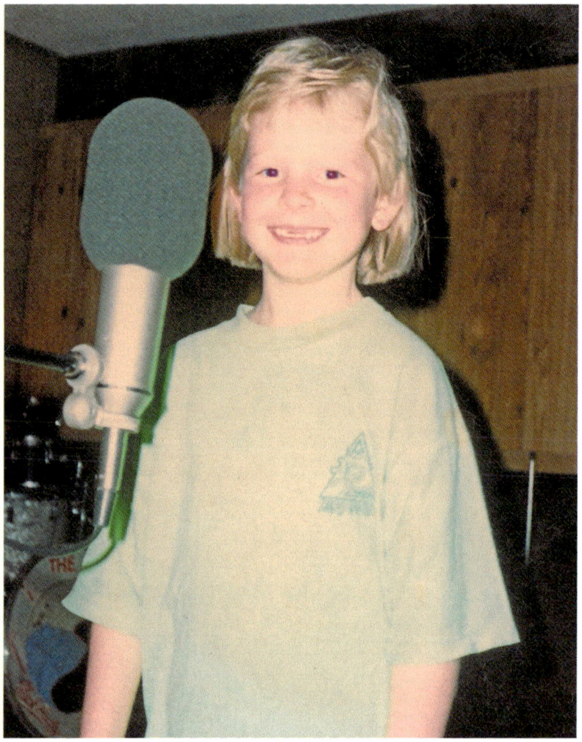

Michelle recording "The Lord Detests Lying Lips"

I was especially thrilled that Merry had decided to record Jonny's special song, *"For God has not given us a spirit of fear but of power and of love and of a sound mind." 2 Timothy 1.7*

As happened after every recording, Merry was completely exhausted. For months she had been training children and working with various talented and temperamental musicians to bring to pass the music she could hear in her head. She had done a fantastic job, and the backing tracks were amazing. Now she needed to take a break. What better way than the gift of a house boat holiday cruising the inlets of Surfers' Paradise for a week!

Chapter 9:

The House Boat Holiday

*"Every good gift and every perfect gift is from above and cometh down from the Father."
James 1:17 (KJV) Children Arise Vol 5.*

*"Those who trust in the Lord are as steady as Mount Zion, unmoved by any circumstance."
Psalm 125.1(TLB) Children Arise Vol 1.*

"Rejoice evermore! Pray without ceasing, in everything give thanks for this is the will of God in Christ Jesus concerning you." 1 Thessalonians 5:16-18 (KJV) Children Arise Vol 2.

Wow! We were pinching ourselves to make sure this was real!

It was the final week of our stay in Brisbane, and God was blessing both the Billing family and the Targett family through a wonderful Christian couple who owned and operated large house boats on the Gold Coast. They had offered us all the use of one of their biggest and best house-boats, free of charge for one week. These kind people knew how busy we had all been, particularly the Billings. Our children could hardly believe this amazing treat!

As we all excitedly filed onto our luxurious 'home away from home', we all recognised once again God's goodness and kindness to us all. Although this gift of a holiday was being offered to us by a wonderful Christian couple, we knew God had prompted them to bless us all in this wonderful way, and we were experiencing the reality of the verse, *"Every good gift and every perfect gift is from above and cometh down from the Father." James 1. 17*

As the children excitedly explored their new accommodation, Graeme and Paul read the operation manual and nervously began to work out how to drive the huge boat. Meanwhile Merry and I oohed and aahed over the luxurious surroundings. Every day for a lovely long week our combined families of four adults and five children cruised in and around the estuaries surrounding Surfers Paradise. What a dream holiday! We would remember this for many years to come.

The fourth and final week of our Brisbane trip was one of the most exciting we had all experienced. We all thanked God daily for this beautiful holiday, and the opportunity to wind down and relax after such a busy time recording.

Graeme and Paul soon mastered the art of steering our house boat. We visited the island of Courang Cove, and the children had a fantastic time jumping off the sides of thc boat and swimming in the warm surrounding waters.

By the end of this amazing week we all felt totally refreshed. Graeme had also agreed to produce the manual for parents that I had been working on for the last few months. Six months before, God had been prompting me to spend half a day each week at the local library while He gave me the plan for a practical manual for parents and the idea for a course that would later be called 'Raising Children God's Way'. The manual would complement the Children Arise CDs. This manual would teach the practical application of the Scriptures being put to music for other families to use.

From top: Janine, Merrilyn, Christopher, Michelle and Carolyn
enjoying the House Boat Holiday

This manual was very dear to my heart, and I knew God had opened the door for publication when Graeme agreed to produce it along with a music book for both Children Arise Volumes 1 and 2. I had spent many, many hours trying to put these songs into written music. They were in my head and on my tape recorder but not on paper. After doing my best, and sending them all up to Brisbane, the written music was finally produced by other more capable musicians, to my great relief, and plans for production of the music book were already well underway so that other families could play the tunes on piano, keyboard, or guitar.

I knew this Manual was a part of God's plan to make a practical tool available to parents so their children could also learn to apply these Scriptures in their lives. To me this Manual was the other half of the package, which would be placed in the hands of families everywhere. Already God was confirming in many ways that this concept - produced and packaged so beautifully by Merry and Graeme - would be sent around the world. At the time of writing, Children Arise music and material is now in eleven countries around the world.

To our little family it was the icing on the cake at the end of an exciting month when Graeme accepted my manual notes and promised to have it produced in the coming months along with the music book. The songs God had given to our family were about to be made available on a wider scale through the amazing giftedness of the Billing family.

Our holiday was now over. Time to go home! With grateful hearts we thanked our kind house boat owners and made our way back to Brisbane, ready to make the trip back home to Tasmania the next day.

Unbelievably the pilot strike was still on, (after a whole month!) The next day we arrived at the airport only to be told "Sorry! No planes travelling today! Try again tomorrow!" We spent an extra, final and very special evening with the Billings, before once again preparing for the exciting adventure back to Tasmania.

The day had arrived! We had been officially booked on a return flight to Melbourne on another huge Jumbo Jet – much to the excitement of our children. Once again, we were to find it would not be straightforward.

As Paul showed our tickets at one counter he was told "Sorry Sir, you will be required to pay an extra $850 to get back to Tasmania." In dismay he came back to confer with us all, and once again our family and the Billings went into a small huddle there in the middle of the Brisbane airport and asked God to please show us what to do next as we didn't have $850 to pay – we had spent all our money by this stage.

As we finished praying I glanced across to another counter and suggested Paul show our tickets to the man standing there. To our total amazement and relief he nodded and beckoned us all through without any word at all of extra cost. With sighs of relief we waved to the Billing family and hurried to our departure lounge. Within a short time we had boarded another Jumbo Jet. What a memory for our children!

This time the flight went straight through to Melbourne, and after a short wait we were again boarding a strange looking Hercules army plane. As Andrea, Jonny and Michelle were strapped tightly into the bare seats facing each other, they were handed plastic lunch boxes of food by real live army guys, much to their delight. As the plane took off with a deafening roar, Paul and I grinned at each other and agreed that this had to be one of the most amazing adventures we had EVER had as a family!

While thousands of people had cancelled trips and holidays, God had enabled the five of us to travel to the other end of the country and back, and witness the production of, and participate in, the recording of Children Arise Volume two.

Michelle's solo and the photos of our children on the cover of the new CD were proof that we had done the impossible! While everyone said it "couldn't be done!" with God's help we had done it anyway.

"Those who trust in the Lord are as steady as Mount Zion unmoved by any circumstance."

– Psalm 25:1 (KJV) Children Arise Vol. 1

Chapter 10:

The Shack Mess

"If your enemy is hungry give him food to eat. If he is thirsty give him water to drink. In doing this you will heap burning coals on his head and the Lord will reward you." Proverbs 25:21,22 (NIV) (unrecorded)

"But I say unto you that hear, love your enemies, do good to them that hate you, bless them that curse you and pray for them that despitefully use you."

Luke 6:27, 28 (KJV). Children Arise Vol,3

It just wasn't right. It wasn't fair! I looked in dismay at the figures in our bank balance.

Another week had gone by, and still no rent had been paid into our account by the lady who was renting our holiday home. We had been back from our Brisbane holiday for some months now, and money was still rather tight. We had spent our extra savings on a beautiful set of family portraits and a new set of cases now that we all had the 'travel bug', so we really needed that extra avenue of income to keep the bills paid on both homes. During these years Paul and I had made a conscious decision that I would be home with the children, so his wage was our sole source of income. At times our finances were quite tight, yet God always seemed to bless us for that decision.

Although we all called it 'the shack', it was really a nice little three bedroom cottage at Low Head, near two beautiful beaches; Lagoon Bay and East Beach, in Northern Tasmania. To help cover expenses we were renting it through the year to a lady and her two teenage children.

It was now seven weeks since a repayment had gone into our account and despite repeated calls and a letter sent, there was still no payment! Our 'shack lady' was fast becoming a squatter!

What a challenge. With my strong sense of injustice I was becoming quite an aggravation to our family with my exasperated, angry comments as the weeks went by. The verse the children were learning at that time presented me with a challenge. Could I put this into practice? *"If your enemy is hungry give him food to eat, if he is thirsty give him water to drink. In doing this you will heap burning coals on his head and the Lord will reward you."*

We had no way of knowing if this lady was hungry and couldn't afford the rent or not, but she was fast becoming my enemy!

Paul decided a trip to Low Head was necessary to confront our tenant with her lack of payment, so our plan to do things God's way went into action.

We had heard she had moved out and was staying just down the road with her daughter, so we expected there might be some cleaning to do. The car was loaded up with cleaning equipment 'just in case'.

As the children piled into the car for the trip to Low Head they were each carrying a gift for 'the shack lady'. Between them they were carrying a lovely basket of flowers with ribbon bows, homemade ginger snaps done up in cellophane with pretty ribbon, (the results of a family cooking afternoon the day before), and a jar of home-made blackberry jam with a bright fabric cover over the top.

We were determined to bless the lady and her family regardless of their treatment to us.

On the trip down we each prayed for her and her two children and asked God to bless them. Then we took our prayers a step further and asked God to please cause this lady and her children to become Christians at some time in their lives.

As I heard the cute voices of the children praying from the back seat of the car I thought "Wow! – God's ways are so different from the world's ways." I wondered if our children would grow up with a completely different response if injustice was done to them in the future.

Paul had decided we would call first at the daughter's home and speak to our tenant, and then continue on to check out our own holiday home. As we pulled into the daughter's drive way there was a furtive movement behind the curtains in the front room. We discovered later why our tenant was not willing to come out. When the daughter finally answered the door Paul was informed our tenant was 'not there at the moment'. Behind him stood the children and I with our gifts.

As the children and I began to pass the flowers, biscuits and jam over to the girl for her mother, her mouth dropped open and she stared in total shock. She appeared unable to say anything she was so stunned!

Five minutes later, pulling into the driveway of our own little cottage, none of us were prepared for the sight that met our eyes. There was a huge pile of rubbish and household goods sitting outside the front door. Doors slammed as the children, Paul and I began stepping carefully around the loads of rubbish, clothes, toys and even furniture as we made our way into the lounge room.

The place was totally filthy! If the lady had vacated, as her daughter had informed us, then she had left most of her belongings behind. The verse we were putting into practice was, I'm sure, more for me than for our children!

Both Paul and the children knew that my *normal* reaction would have been total outrage at the injustice of what we were seeing. Instead, as they looked at me for my expected response, I was suddenly filled with laughter! I laughed and laughed and laughed – I couldn't stop! I flopped onto the floor laughing, and I could almost hear the audible sighs of relief as the children observed my 'God given' reaction to such a horrible situation. One by one they too began to laugh (at me!) and soon our attitudes were all positive as we spent a good, long, hardworking, but happy family day getting on with the job of evacuating our tenant's property and cleaning and scrubbing each room.

Even the carpet stank, and we all agreed our tenants had obviously kept a pet inside although they had signed an agreement that NO pets were allowed. Yet even that couldn't take away my peace, so Paul and the children didn't complain much either. We were determined to do this God's way, and it had become a family challenge.

Paul, Janine, Michelle and Andrea working on the shack mess

At the end of a long day we all trooped outside to our car to start the drive back home. Miraculously, there were no bad attitudes. We had completed this project as a team. Our shack was now our own again, the clothes, furniture, toys etc. having been deposited on our tenant's daughter's lawn, and, while Paul and I knew we would be *very* careful if we ever rented it out again, we were all happy to have it back and available to be used again.

As we drove home after a happy family day of hard work we agreed that God had shown us a much nicer way to get the job done than any way we would have chosen ourselves. And I knew our family was relieved that I was learning to put God's principles into practice along with them. In the past I had been known to grumble the most at a time like this, but today, only laughter.

We never did hear any more from our 'shack lady', but I knew the experience would be one that our children would take into their adult years and become a new way (God's way) to treat others when any injustice was done to them.

Chapter 11:

THE TEEN YEARS

"Do everything without complaining or arguing, so that you may become blameless and pure, children of God without fault in a crooked and depraved generation in which you shine like stars in the Universe as you hold out the words of life."

Philippians 2:14-16. (NIV) Children Arise Volume 2

It had been the five-to-twelve year window.

Paul and I had discovered there was a 'window of opportunity' when Andrea, Jonny and Michelle were between five years and twelve years. I realised later that if parents were to take full advantage of those years and teach as much Scripture as possible and apply as much as possible, these years could be called the peaceful, delightful years.

They were mostly peaceful, happy years, and, with the habit of obedience well established and Godly principles being learnt and applied continually, family life became a little bit of 'heaven on earth'.

But now it was the 'teenage window!'

The teen years were now approaching, and hormones were going crazy! Suddenly our reasonably obedient, stable, happy children began to complain and argue about all sorts of silly things. It had happened at the two-to-three-year stage, and now it was happening again at the twelve-to-thirteen-year stage.

"Yes Mum!" or "Yes Dad!" were not quite as acceptable to say at this age, and it seemed arguments and complaints were popping up everywhere.

Once again I was thrilled when I discovered a fantastic nugget of wisdom I could hand to our children to show them that complaining and arguing was not just unacceptable to us as parents, but also unacceptable to God. He was encouraging them in His word to "do everything WITHOUT complaining or arguing."

This verse was such a positive one to give the children as a new song:

"Do EVERYTHING without complaining or arguing, so that you may become blameless and pure, children of God without fault in a crooked and depraved generation, in which you shine like stars in the universe as you hold out the words of life."

As we sat one afternoon after school, munching on my ginger nut crunches and relaxing on couches with Jonny (as usual) in a weird position in the bean bag, I announced the fact that I had found some great new instruction for them, and I would sing it to them. What could they say? It was in God's Word. *"Do everything without complaining or arguing."* Well, if God said it, we would try to remind each other to put this new principle into practice. There were grins as I regaled them with a story, I made it up as I went along, about a family of children who constantly argued, bickered and did the 'teenage answer back' thing. As usual, my story was SO much like what was currently happening in our home right then, that the three children could really identify with it. As usual I had no idea how my story was going to finish, so I breathed a huge sigh of relief when my 'arrow prayer' to God, for inspiration was answered, and I as well as the children heard a happy ending. And so began our new week of learning to DO more of God's Word with a practical application called 'no complaining and no arguing!'

Later, when Paul began to write his 'Uncle Paul's Story book', I was so relieved as his stories flowed so effortlessly and were SO much better than my hurried bursts of inspiration and desperation born out of determination that our children would be taught something.

From Parent to Parent

So many times since I have learnt that many parents just do not talk to their children about God AT ALL! Nothing! They hoped their children would somehow catch their beliefs by taking them to church or putting them in Christian schools. But the tragedy with many has been that they don't catch anything, and they are now adult non-Christians beginning a new generation which has turned away from God. They may well be the beginning of many generations to come who know nothing of God at all. So parents – be encouraged. Any teaching is better than no teaching at all!

As our now older children sang (because I made them) this verse daily, and we constantly discussed it, the truth of this teaching began to be applied. To my delight, I found once again the promise given by the visiting speaker years before was again coming to pass, as our teenagers were being *"taught of the Lord and great was the peace of our children." Isaiah 54.13. (Children Arise Vol 1)*

Epilogue to this story

As I write this chapter our children are now busy training their own children. Paul and I have discovered that all those years of training has given our own children a huge love and respect for Scripture, and they all have a big desire to impart that love and knowledge of God's Words into their own families now they are married.

Michelle and Jo; Jonny and Verity each have a toddler and a three year old. Their initial training in obedience is well underway, and they all love the Children Arise songs, which are played each day. Michelle's little girl Caitlyn MUST have 'the songs' before she can settle and sleep at night. So far she has had three years of 'the songs', and she knows most of them by heart. Just yesterday Michelle told me she had started 'Verse Times' with her two children, (soon to be three children) and Caitlyn stood and quoted the Scripture to me, *"And be ye kind one unto another, tender-hearted, forgiving one another, even as God for Christ's sake has forgiven you."* (Children Arise Volume 2.) Michelle had begun to teach that verse so Caitlyn would treat her little brother more kindly! Last week when Caitlyn was having an afternoon nap at 'Nanny's place' I forgot to turn on the CD with her songs. Five minutes later I smiled to myself as I heard the C.D. playing. She had hopped out of bed and turned it on herself.

Jonny's boy, Sonny, loves to sing and dance to 'the songs' as he watches his Dad on the stage at church playing electric guitar. Many times Sonny has had to be escorted off the stage for bouncing and singing songs to Jesus. So instead, he stands on his chair and claps and sings. Toddlers Kipp and Samuel are both being introduced to their parent's love of Scripture in music at a young age.

Andrea and Lynden have eight children ranging in age from six months to eleven years. So far, five of their children are through the 'obedience stage' and it is a delight to hear the "Yes Mum" or "Yes Dad" that comes from them. The older boys, Lucas, Jake and Zachary, have learnt about one hundred and ten Scriptures so far, and, while being typical energetic, rowdy boys, they have a real peace about them and a real relationship with Jesus as their Saviour. Bronte, who is just six informed me recently that she will be getting married later to a man who loves Jesus. She tells everyone who will listen that "Jesus died on the cross for their sins." Andrea's other four children, Seth, twin girls Ava and Jessica and baby Evie are already soaking up the music as they hear verses being sung by the older children.

I am being given the privilege of taking a Monday morning 'Verse Time' with Andrea and Lynden's five eldest children, something I really treasure. At 9.00 a.m. on a Monday morning, Lucas, Jake, Zachary, Bronte and Seth come running across the paddocks from their home on the next property with their 'Verse Time' folders ready to sing and quote the Scripture they have been learning all week with Andrea. After a story relating to the new verse I am teaching, they sing their new verse and receive some activities to take home to reinforce it. (The dot-to-dot verse and the double lined verse to colour in that I used with our own children). 'Verse Time' is more exciting for the grandchildren than it was for our children. Our children only received a sticker at the end of each week – but our beautiful grandchildren can choose a prize out of my present box for correctly singing and quoting their 'last week's verse'.

Bronte, Zachary, Lucas and Jake coming for a Verse Time

As I waited last Monday at the adjoining fence between the two properties (such an amazing blessing!) the children caught sight of me, and Jake began to shout loudly, "Nanny! I know the verse!" "Do not merely listen to the Word and so deceive yourselves, DO what it says!" Six-year old Bronte, being piggy backed by her big brother Lucas was not to be outdone, so she began to shout too. "Nanny! I know the verse as well!" *"Do not merely listen to the Word and so deceive yourselves, DO what it says!"* As they arrived with lots of hugs and kisses and sat in a little row on the couches near our piano it took me back to the many, many, many times when Andrea, Jonny and Michelle had done the same thing, and now – what a blessing! Here was the next generation. Thank you Andrea and Lynden for such a privilege.

Paul and I are so thrilled to be a part of the lives of the next generation as we watch them learning to sing, say and DO God's Words. Already Michelle's little Caitlyn has been set free from fear of flies by constantly quoting *"God has not given me a spirit of fear but of power and of love and of a sound mind."* Andrea's Jake was such a fearful toddler that Andrea had him quoting the same verse night after night for about a year, and now, as a nine year old he is a boisterous, fearless and confident boy. God's words are working in this new generation.

Paul and I pray for our grandchildren regularly that they will all grow up to be strong Christians, marry Christian husbands and wives, and continue the next generation with good strong Christian families.

Chapter 12:

Grandma's Story

"Cast your burdens upon the Lord and he shall sustain Thee. He will never suffer the righteous to be moved." Psalm 55:22 (KJV) Children Arise Volume 4.

As the children did their usual Wednesday afternoon jobs for Grandma, I sat chatting to her and enjoying a cup of tea and one of her famous lemon slices. Jonny grinned cheekily at us from the outside of the window he was cleaning. Michelle sat at the kitchen table polishing Grandma's silver tea-pot, milk jug and sugar bowl, while Andrea did her regular job of carefully dusting all of Grandma's precious ornaments, vases, tiny collectables and mirrors. Wednesday afternoon was the time the children had their piano lessons, and, over the last few years it had also become a 'jobs for Grandma' afternoon. Now, as Grandma sat busily knitting a jumper for Jonny she sighed and said quietly, "I don't think I can take much more Jan!"

Paul's mother – known to us all as Grandma Targett - was a saintly Salvation Army lady, who was loved and respected by us all. She had just received news of the accidental death of the son of one of her very good friends, and as this was the third piece of sad news in one week - her compassionate heart for others felt like it was breaking.

Grandma was an amazing woman and a wonderful example to our children of a godly older woman. Although quite frail as a result of operations for cancer, she was an amazing example of a woman who drew her strength from God on a daily basis.

As she sat quietly knitting, I began to daydream.

Years before – when our children were quite small – I remembered asking her what her secret was, because she seemed to achieve more than two or three women combined. She said "Jan, I pray all the time." I knew then that she lived life to the fullest because she placed her hand in God's hand and walked and talked with Him about everything. Even now as a now frail little lady in her seventies, Grandma's weekly achievements were incredible. She played the cello in the Launceston orchestra, having done so for the last thirty years, playing in local musicals and concerts throughout the year. Her orchestra practice was always Wednesday night, and she had a regular Monday morning ensemble practice with three friends.

Sundays were always amazing! She began the morning by putting on a roast dinner for between ten and fifteen of her family members – including our family. This was a family tradition we had had since our children were very small. Next she would be transported by a friend to play the piano at Tyler House old people's home for their morning church service. Then it was off to the Salvation Army service where she was also the pianist.

At lunch time she came home to serve lunch to her family and often tea as well if they stayed all afternoon, then back to church at night, often with guests coming to supper to share one of her famous pavlovas.

Grandma Targett on her way to visit patients in hospital.

What an inspiration Grandma was to us all! Throughout the week she would wear her Salvation Army uniform and visit every one in the local hospital by herself. It was many years before she finally found some other ladies willing to help her. She often had pyjamas on her clothes-line that she'd kindly washed for people she met during her hospital visits, people who had no-one to look after them. Many of them thought she was a saint, and wrote and visited her for years afterwards.

Because Grandma had had two mastectomies and a hysterectomy through cancer, she was asked to join a small group of women who counselled other women having similar operations. She was such an inspiration to those women as she showed them there was 'life after cancer'.

Throughout each week Grandma also went to ladies Home League meetings every Tuesday afternoon, accompanied and led a small singing group on piano on Thursday mornings and went to her Friendship Bible Study Thursday evenings.

Grandma Targett playing her much loved cello

She still somehow managed to show her love for her husband and family of three boys, and their wives and children, by knitting amazingly colourful 'fair-isle' jumpers for nearly all of them each year, while her hospitality, cooking and house keeping skills were also amazing.

A true Proverbs 31 woman. And what a great role model for her daughter-in-law!

I knew then, when Grandma said she didn't know if she could take much more, it was not the many things that went to make up her life, but because her heart was so soft and kind towards so many that she was taking on too many burdens for the people around her. My daydreaming was interrupted as Grandma spoke again. "Jan," she said, "I was looking through my promise box the other day and I pulled out this verse. It has been such a help to me." She read it out. *"Cast thy burdens upon the Lord and He shall sustain thee. He shall never suffer the righteous to be moved." Psalm 55:22.*

I suddenly had some inspiration. Surely God could give us a beautiful tune for this verse as a gift to Grandma.

I quickly copied it down, and two days later I brought it back to her on a cassette tape, a gift of her special verse sung by her three grandchildren. Grandma was so thrilled!

God used this verse as a gentle reminder to her that her secret had always been to cast her burdens on Him and He would sustain her. As she began to do this again, He did sustain her, and she continued to be our beautiful example of a godly older woman.

When my sister Merry produced Children Arise volume 4, it was with great delight that I presented her with her very own copy of her special verse, with beautiful accompaniment from a Grand Piano, which Merry had organised to be bought into the studio, an instrument so special to Grandma!

This verse became our tribute to Grandma. God continued to take the burdens she handed to Him and He sustained her, giving her a full and fulfilled life to the age of eighty-five years.

Chapter 13:

TO REBEL OR NOT TO REBEL

"Morning by morning Oh lord you hear my voice, morning by morning I lay my requests before you and wait in expectation."

Psalm 5:3 (KJV). Children Arise Volume 5.

Andrea walked into the lounge room. "Mum, I want to rebel!"

Andrea was in Grade 9. She was now fourteen. With a stubborn, determined look on her face she repeated her statement to me, "Mum, I want to rebel!"

Her friends were going to parties each Friday night and wanting her to come. The parties were where the drinking and smoking was happening, and I knew one friend in particular had the potential to pull Andrea right away from her relationship with God. Andrea informed me that all the 'cool kids' went to the parties, and she wanted to be in the 'cool' group.

At that time the High School teenagers were either going to Youth Groups or parties on a Friday night. For the last couple of years Paul and I had been running a relaxed style Youth Group in our home, mainly because the official Youth Group leader had suddenly given up the job and there was no-one to facilitate one. Because Andrea and Jonny were both Youth Group age (High School) we had agreed to become facilitators the first year by taking the group to the homes of different parents of our group and asking them to provide supper and some form of activity, while Paul did a study each week. We had no intention of becoming 'Youth Group Leaders' ourselves and just looked at the job of being facilitators so that our children had some-where to go each Friday night. Little did we know that we would continue running this group in our own home for the next fourteen years! As parents Paul and I took her comment quite seriously, and began to pray for wisdom. Our answer came from a book by Anne Ortland called 'Disciplines of the Heart' where Anne told of a short Bible study and prayer time she had had with each of her four children every morning, Now each adult child had a huge love of God's Word and most were in Christian ministry of some sort.

Her plan was simple so we began.

Andrea and I took twenty minutes at a set time each morning, and met in the lounge room from 6.10 to 6.30 am. I had worked out that Andrea loved quality time, (it was her love language), so when I told her of my plan she was quite happy. She was an early riser and loved to be orderly and have a plan for the day so she agreed to try our new mother/daughter time.

On the first morning I found Andrea sitting in our lounge room pointing to her watch when I arrived. Secretly I was thrilled that she had taken the new suggestion so seriously. We sat with our Bibles, a notebook and pen, and began to put into practice the verse quoted above. We began with 1 Corinthians chapter 1. I had chosen to start with this book of the Bible because the apostle Paul had such a lot of wisdom and common sense in his teachings, and I had found so much good advice on how to successfully live the Christian life that might be applicable to our own teenagers. The idea was to begin the new program with Andrea and see how we went.

By now she was impatient to begin, so we followed Anne Ortland's plan, and Andrea read verse 1, I read verse 2 and we continued alternating through the chapter. We repeated this process, only this time it was my turn to begin. We then spent five or ten minutes quietly sitting putting pen to paper and summarizing what we had just read, choosing two or three important points that had made an impact on us and writing them down as well.

We shared our summaries out loud and then had a short time sharing prayer points for each other for the day. It was such a peaceful, positive time, and we both enjoyed it so much we decided to continue each school morning.

So the pattern was set. As we daily worked our way through 1 Corinthians, God began to show Andrea through His Word that rebellion really wasn't such a good idea at all. God's absolutes were set out in the Scriptures we read. Andrea could clearly see God's ways and the ways of the world, and the difference between the two.

This time for us became the pattern we set for the next six years until Andrea married Lynden at the age of twenty. By the time Jonny, and later, Michelle reached the age of fourteen or fifteen, I had three twenty minute time slots scheduled for each of them, and went from room to room. 6.10: Andrea, 6.30: Michelle and 6.50: Jonny. For a while Paul took Jonny's time slot, but when I caught the pair of them sitting back snoozing against their pillows a few mornings in a row I decided Paul's input in the evenings was so much more helpful, and he was much more wide awake by then!

Jonathan as a teenager trying to stay awake for an early morning Bible study with Dad

As well as our afternoon Verse Time (mainly just singing and discussing a weekly verse), God taught our children in this way through their teen years, and by the time each had turned twenty they had all summarized most of the New Testament and prayed for the salvation of many of their friends during our prayer times. We became great prayer partners, and praying became a very natural extension of our communication.

As a result they each moved into their twenties with a big heart for others, a big love for God and His Word, and a desire to make a difference in the world around them. Also, by the time they reached adulthood they had all experienced so many answers to prayers. They knew that as they laid their requests before God each morning and waited in expectation that He would answer. Many wonderful miracles were documented in their morning study books. To this day I still have each of their study books as special treasures. Are all mothers this sentimental?

Andrea found she was unable to rebel… she had learnt and put into practice too many Scriptures over the years to be able to really move too far away from God. It reminded me of the Pastor I had heard preaching at Rhema Family Church in Perth, Western Australia, a few years earlier. He said, "I tried to rebel during my teen years but my Mum had taught me too many Scriptures and I couldn't do it! And now…. Here I am. A pastor!"

I also found from a mother's viewpoint, that this time of commitment of twenty minutes quality time through the teen years, was one of the best ways to help get our children's personal faith and trust in God to become firmly established. They could then move into adulthood with their lives on a firm foundation. One of the best rewards of putting Anne Ortland's idea into practice was that it provided a personal communication time. This probably could not have been achieved on a daily basis any other way through those often hectic, busy, teenage years.

Paul had his important input into the lives of our teenagers by establishing a pattern every evening of a Bible reading, discussion and prayer time around our table for any problems our children were experiencing. The tea-time communication was so popular and often so noisy that it was quite hard to get a word in. Those teenage years became a time of great communication, lots of prayer for each other, and somehow all three children seemed to miss out on that dreaded 'teenage rebellion' that so many parents are fearful of.

However, no parent has perfect children and no parent is perfect either, so there were more stories to come, and Andrea's story continues into the next three chapters.

From Parent to Parent

Paul and I have since observed how important it is that parents daily *speak* to their children about God and pray with them. Just living a good Christian life in front of their children is not enough. There must be communication as well. In later years many of our children's friends loved coming to tea to experience the noisy communication, care and prayer at our family meal times.

Today, with the children all married, we have Monday evenings as an open home for any of them to come with their children and share a roast meal, love, laughter, conversation, and our usual Bible reading and prayer time. It is even noisier now than it was back then! Since Nanna Austin (my mum) passed away five years ago, my father (Grandad Austin) has enjoyed our Monday night roast each week, and as he comes to the back door, he checks the welcome sign on the blackboard to see how many of the children and grandchildren will be coming to tea that night. He totally delights in being a part of our now extended family, and, many a night he gives a passionate mini-sermon over tea, and prays fervently with us for any current needs.

Although Paul and I had just three children we are so blessed that our current family count is now twenty-one, with thirteen beautiful grandchildren. Verity, a beautiful godly daughter-in law and wife for Jonny, and Lynden and Joseph, two tall, handsome godly sons-in law for Andrea and Michelle. N.B. All of our amazing and special in-laws received at least ten good years of prayer from our children as they prayed through the teen years for their future husbands and wife. Each prayed quite regularly for God's protection on their future partner, and that they would be a strong Christian. This was one of the prayers that we prayed regularly during our early morning prayer times and, as a result, there were many years of thanking God for just the right partner for each of them. Through those years the following verse became a special song:

"Be ye not unequally yoked together with unbelievers, for what fellowship hath righteousness with unrighteousness, and what communion hath light with darkness."

2 Corinthians 6:14 (KJV) (Unrecorded)

But back to ''The Stories behind the Songs' and our next chapter, 'The Sorting Out Prayer'.

Lynden & Andrea

Jonathan & Verity

Michelle & Joseph

Paul and Janine with their children and grandchildren

Chapter 14:

THE 'SORTING OUT' PRAYER

"But I say unto you that hear, love your enemies, do good to them that hate you, bless them that curse you and pray for them that despitefully use you." Luke 6:27,28 (KJV) Children Arise. Vol 3.

"But if you forgive men when they sin against you your heavenly father will also forgive you. But if you do not forgive men their sins your father will not forgive your sins." Matthew 6:14,15 (KJV) (unrecorded)

"Jesus said, "Father, forgive them for they do not know what they are doing." Luke 23:34 (a) (KJV)

"If we confess our sins He is faithful and just to forgive us our sins and to cleanse us from all unrighteousness."1 John 1:19 (KJV) (unrecorded)

Wow! What an exciting key for our family, and all of our friends, as it turned out later. This discovery became one of the most important in the lives of our whole family and in the lives of many, many of our friends.

On the recommendation of a good friend I had just bought the book 'Power Manual' by June Newman Davies and it was a powerhouse of ideas! (Most of my ideas came from books.) June Newman Davies had also written 'Scripture Keys for Kingdom Living', and I loved it because it consisted of lists of Scriptures for every occasion. Now, as I read the book 'Power Manual' and had just finished the chapter titled 'Tri-lateral Forgiveness', I was having a huge light bulb moment. This chapter was the most amazing key I had ever come across to help enable people to REALLY forgive properly.

I had come from a family of very strong temperaments, and, during my own teen years, the words "I'm sorry" were not in my vocabulary. I had come into my marriage to Paul not knowing how to say "I'm sorry," nor how to forgive and forget grievances. I had observed members of my extended family who had an amazing ability to remember every grievance that had occurred over a number of years – these things played out in their minds as clearly as though they had happened yesterday. One relative in particular was known by the family as a bitter man. Nearly every word that came from his mouth was full of bitterness, anger and un-forgiveness towards others. He was unhappy, and we felt so sorry for his wife and children who were being brought up in that negative environment. How would it affect them in years to come?

Although we all had a strong protective love for each other, the saying that blood's thicker than water was definitely true. I remembered how much strife had occurred amongst my siblings because of our inability to forgive and forget. I had made a conscious decision that I didn't want this trait in our children. I especially didn't want our children to grow up and come back to us to tell us of all the things we had done wrong through their lives. I had seen enough of that behaviour in other adults that I felt very determined we would all learn (somehow) to keep short accounts with each other.

And now, here was the key: Tri-lateral forgiveness. Or three-way forgiveness.

As I read, I realized these principles could be simplified for our children, so I called it 'The Sorting Out Prayer'.

This prayer was so simple, yet so profound. Our children wrote it out on three pieces of cardboard in nice bright colours, and pinned it to the noticeboards that Paul had made for each of them. This prayer was now on display in their bedrooms, and was to remain there for the next few years.

June Newman Davies explained that this prayer was such a thorough way to learn the art of forgiveness, that, by the time the person prayed the final prayer asking God to bless the one who had ill treated them, the person praying was completely set free from the previous anger, hatred and upset. They were 'SORTED OUT!' They could then get on with life and leave the grievance behind. (At this time of writing every member of our family has verbally prayed this prayer many, many, many times –some of us a lot more than others, depending on our temperaments. Andrea and I probably have the highest count at this point in time.)

Two comments Andrea wrote to me recently as a young adult when she presented me with a beautiful book titled, "Mother, thank you for…" say it all!

"How many times did you have to sit on the end of my bed for a very long time until I decided to forgive?"

"I have no emotional baggage to lug around so life is pretty stable. It feels great!"

This was the prayer as Andrea, Jonny and Michelle wrote it out:

The Sorting Out Prayer

1. **I forgive............................for........................ (Matthew 6:14,15)**
2. **Dear God please forgive................for ....(Luke 23: 34)**
3. **Please forgive me for getting angry. (1 John 1: 9)**
4. **Please take all the anger and upset out of me. (1 John 1: 9)**
5. **Please bless.................................... (Luke 6: 27,28)**

Although the practical application of this amazing prayer is told in the next chapter, 'Thanks Mum! Whoops! I forgot again', this one prayer became one of the most powerful tools our family used over the years. It kept us free from resentment, kept our forgiveness up to date, and it helped create an environment for strong and healthy emotional growth in each of our children.

Many, many friends were given copies of this prayer by each of us at different times, and, without exception, when our friends were able to sincerely pray a blessing (step 5) over the person who had wronged them they were totally set free from ALL anger and resentment no matter HOW badly they had been wronged. Sometimes the prayer of blessing needed to be continued on behalf of the other, but it always brought amazing results of freedom for the one who prayed.

Personally, this prayer has become one of the keys to a very happy marriage, and I am quite sure that if I too had not put this prayer into practice, I may well have become one of the 'bitter' ones in my family line. Instead, Paul has had the blessing of a wife who is only allowed to stay angry or hold a grudge for a VERY short time – thanks to the reminders of our three children!

Chapter 15:

THANKS MUM! WHOOPS! I FORGOT AGAIN!

"In your anger do not sin, do not let the sun go down while you are still angry and do not give the devil a foothold." Ephesians 4:26,27 (KJV). Children Arise Vol 2

"I just wanted to thank you Mum!"

"What for Andrea?"

"For teaching me to sort myself out and forgive people."

Andrea was calling out to me from her bedroom.

She was now fifteen. It was summer holidays, and we were staying at our shack at Low Head. It was about ten o'clock at night and both Jonny and Michelle were in bed reading, this was one of our favourite past times at the shack.

"Mum!" Andrea was calling again.

As I sat on the end of her bed and listened to her thanking me, I was thrilled. After all those years of working with Andrea, helping her deal with anger problems, I thought, "we've made it! Hoorah! Our 'Sorting out prayer' is working!" She was so grateful that night for all she had learnt about forgiving others.

That summer holiday was a lovely time of fun, friendship and family. It was idyllic. The days over that five weeks were spent on all our favourite holiday activities – swimming, bike riding, long walks, reading as many books as we could take home from the local library, shopping for treats, barbecues, surfing (for Paul and Jonny), body boarding for the rest of us, climbing sand dunes and racing or rolling back down them, and lots of friends and family calling unexpectedly for a day at the beach with the Targetts.

But this story is not so much about that idyllic year as it is about the following year.

Parents never relax and think you've made it. A year later, again at the shack, it was a different story…

Andrea was NOT happy! Up until that time we had been having our daily Bible Study together, but because she had been so busy with her Year 10 work we had missed the last couple of months before our holidays. As a result we had not been praying together as we usually did, so we had missed that quality time that was so important to Andrea.

This year Andrea was sixteen years old, Jonny was fourteen and Michelle was twelve, and on this holiday we were all being totally lazy. It was wonderful! (I thought). We could all sleep in, read books and relax.

However, Andrea was becoming more moody each day - she didn't want to do anything we wanted to do.

This year she didn't like sand.

She didn't feel like riding her bike.

She didn't want to go swimming.

She didn't want to do anything! Just sit and read, or frown and snap at us.

This went on for most of the five weeks we were staying at our shack, and for some reason it didn't occur to me what the problem might be. I guess not having had a sixteen year old before I thought it must be something that happened when your teenager reached that age!

Funny isn't it? You can work on problems for years and, when they crop up again, you don't even see them. But this particular evening I'd had enough. Paul happened to be away that night as he had been called back to work, so Andrea was using that as an opportunity to give me a hard time. Jonny and Michelle had just gone off to bed and Andrea made a sarcastic comment to me. Suddenly something inside me snapped! My own bossy choleric nature came to the fore and I said loudly "RIGHT! I've had enough of this. Just wait there!" Suddenly all became clear. I charged off into the kitchen, grabbed a writing pad and pen and went back in and said, "Andrea. I want you to write down every single thing you are angry about and I'll be back in ten minutes!" I walked out and shut the door and went into the lounge to try and cool off a bit, because by that time I was very angry myself.

While I waited I had to sort myself out. Having taught the 'Sorting out Prayer' for so many years I realised I couldn't expect Andrea to pray and forgive if I wasn't willing to do it myself. So, with my own heart pounding I prayed a quick prayer forgiving and blessing Andrea so I could be in the right frame of mind to help her get her own attitude sorted out.

I went back in to Andrea's room to find, to my surprise, that she had been writing solidly since I'd left. She had written twenty-one points down, and covered a whole page in bright red writing! As she handed me the sheet of paper I could see that these twenty one points went back over two months, and her many grievances had probably blown out of all proportion since we had stopped communicating and praying together. I gulped as I realised that the majority of points Andrea had written down concerned me!

There were things that I'd said or done or hadn't done over the last eight weeks or so. Some things were just a sentence which had been spoken. For example one of her points was a sentence I had said six weeks before! I had completely forgotten, but she hadn't, and it was still having the same upsetting effect on her that it had had six weeks ago.

So. I had a job to do.

The next two and a half hours I went through the 'Sorting out Prayer' twenty one times! But first I had to listen to every single point in great detail. I had to hear the whole story as to why each word or incident had upset Andrea. I was so grateful I had the time, because if I hadn't taken time these hurts and grievances would have continued to snowball and become an even bigger problem. Andrea knew of course what she was going to have to do, but already I could see she was relieved because she finally had the opportunity to receive some individual attention. So we began, one point at a time.

At the beginning Andrea was a bit teary, but half way through the long list her expression began to change. The moody sullen look began to disappear, and as we continued down the list discussing, forgiving, and praying blessings on those who had wronged her, she began to look quite angelic. Each time Andrea prayed

I would also pray a short prayer thanking God for taking the upset and anger from her and for freeing her from any foothold the devil may have taken. Her eyes shone, and she had a sweet glow all over her face. We gave each other a big hug and I felt like I had my lovely daughter back again. I had had to apologize quite a few times for my own part in upsetting her, and I had to ask many times "will you forgive me?" When she had finished praying she was a completely different girl!

The next morning Andrea could be heard whistling in the kitchen. After all those weeks of being so unmotivated she was now cutting out fabric and making herself a new dress as she listened to a lovely praise tape. When Jonny and Michelle wandered out for breakfast they were so pleased to have their fun sister back.

Over the next two or three days the sewing machine hummed and the praise music played as she made some artistic outfits, and was back to being the Andrea we all knew and loved.

Those final few days at the shack were so stress free and fun filled that I realised all over again, how important it was for each of us to keep ourselves accountable to one another as a family, and make sure we kept the communication open at all times. The rewards were so worthwhile.

Andrea's story continues in the next chapter.

Andrea happily sewing at the shack.
Next page are two of her award winning designs.

Two of her award winning designs.

From Parent to Parent

This experience impacted Andrea so much that she began to strongly encourage many of her friends to keep their forgiveness up to date, and keep healthy and sweet.

Her sewing hobby, which began in earnest during those holidays at the shack, became an amazingly creative gift, which won her the Fashion Design of the Year Award at the age of eighteen. As I later watched her walking across the stage at a local fashion parade in a spectacular gown she had designed and made herself, I felt so proud of Andrea, and her future career was now stretching ahead of her as she spent the two years before her marriage doing a Diploma in Design and Dress-making.

As her Mum, I was (and still am) the fortunate recipient of many gorgeous outfits designed and made by Andrea, and her creative talents with fabric continue to be used to bless others and to help create a beautiful home for her very large family.

Andrea and I also continued our Bible Studies and prayer times till the age of eighteen, and then became prayer partners (still early in the morning), until she married Lynden at the age of twenty. Now she is married with children, we are better friends than ever, and I see that the strong temperament God gifted her with has made her very capable of running a large family.

Chapter 16:

Punched in the Head

"But I say unto you that hear, love your enemies, do good to them that hate you, bless them that curse you and pray for them that despitefully use you."

Luke 6:27,28 (KJV) Children Arise Vol.3

"Andrea's been punched in the head!"

"WHAT?" I exclaimed.

Andrea had just turned seventeen, and she was about to experience a frightening incident. Paul and I were at the shack for the weekend with Jonny and Michelle. Andrea had decided to stay in town because she wanted to go to church Sunday and see all her friends. She was staying with my sister, Mandie.

That Sunday evening Our Pastor was speaking on the subject of anger and forgiveness, and Andrea had thought to herself, "Well, at least I don't have a problem with that!"

However, as the Pastor continued preaching there was a fellow sitting up the back of the church who had been in and out of psychiatric wards, and had huge problems with anger. Suddenly it became too much for him – he could stand it no longer. He sprang up from his seat, walked over to where Andrea sat near the aisle, and, before most people had even seen or had any idea what had happened, he punched Andrea in the side of her head then turned to walk out of the church.

Immediately it was bedlam! One of Andrea's friends sprang up with a shout and threatened to punch the guy. He was quickly escorted outside by the elders of the church. They had not seen the incident, and wondered what on earth was happening. Then a lady sitting nearby who had seen what had happened raced to Andrea's side and began to whisper reassurances and pray quietly for her.

Andrea later told me her own account. "Suddenly I felt a huge blow to my head, and saw the look of anger and rage on the fellow's face." She continued. "Immediately, like clockwork, my mind clicked into gear, and I began to forgive the guy – praying automatically that God would forgive him and bless him, and I just sat there praying over and over that God would bless him."

As a result, the incident didn't traumatise her at all, and, apart from her head being slightly sore for a day or two, she didn't have any bruising or any other bad effects.

When Paul and I arrived back in town later that evening to collect Andrea from my sister's home, Mandie told us that Andrea had been hit in the head that night during church.

"WHAT!" I exclaimed. "Mum!" said Andrea quietly, looking quite calm and peaceful, "I forgave him!" "Oh!" I said. Well! That deflated me. What else could I say? It looked as though I was about to be more traumatised than my daughter, unless I could follow her example!

During the following week we realised this incident had been a test to the whole church. Many people phoned us, and there were suggestions that we had every right to take the fellow to court.

However, to Andrea, it was now a complete non-issue. So much so, that Paul and I felt as though she had passed an amazing test, and were so proud of her. Andrea had been using the 'Sorting out Prayer', our special prayer of forgiveness, so many times through her teen years that it was obviously now a completely automatic response to negative behaviour from others.

It was so special to observe, ten years after I had first received our special promise that God Himself would teach our children, the fulfilment of that promise in Andrea's life, God had turned one of Andrea's weak points into one of her greatest strengths. Where once it may have taken her a whole lifetime to forgive and forget such an incident, now she knew how to instantly be released from all negative effects of the injustice. Instead she had turned that situation around immediately in a positive way through her request for God to bless the one who had harmed her in such a vicious way.

From Parent to Parent

As I write this story Andrea is now a calm, stable, happy wife and the mother of eight beautiful children. Number eight has recently arrived and she is blessed to have four girls and four boys. Her old sense of injustice and anger is all a thing of the past. Negative situations are turned into blessings as Andrea uses her keys of forgiveness and her prayers of blessing to free and bless those she comes in contact with.

> *Isaiah 54.13 "And all Thy children shall be taught of the Lord and great shall be the peace of thy children." (KJV) Children Arise Vol.1*

Chapter 17:

The Chocolate Cake

"And be ye kind one unto another, tender hearted, forgiving one another, even as God for Christ's sake has forgiven you."

Ephesians 4:32 (KJV)

"If your enemy is hungry give him food to eat, if he is thirsty give him water to drink, in doing this you will heap burning coals on his head and the Lord will reward you."

Proverbs 25: 21, 22 (NIV) (Unrecorded)

"Mum! You have to make Mrs. Barnes a nice chocolate cake!"

Uggh! My daughter may just as well have punched me in the solar plexus. Make Mrs. Barnes a chocolate cake? Why! That lady had caused me more stress and trouble in the last twelve months than anyone had in a long, long time.

For a minute I tried to kid myself that I was just hearing things. Andrea was joking, of course. But no. There she was, her feet planted very firmly in front of me, glint of determination in her eyes and her hands firmly on her hips.

In the past, as her mother, I had been known to display that same determined attitude if I was convinced she should do something a particular way, and now I recognised that same strong determination coming *my* way!

Over the past eighteen months, Andrea, along with the rest of my family, had been observing my own determination, and often great stress. I'd gone from being a Scripture teacher in a local Primary school, to a co-ordinator of fourteen teachers in that same school. When I realised our lovely Bible-based curriculum was at great risk of being replaced by a very secular curriculum – not only in our school but in every other public school – I entered a battlefield, and was gradually elected to every committee in place at the time to discuss this change. Eventually I ended up on the 'Working Group Committee', the 'Heads of Churches Committee', (as a representative of my Pastor and our church movement), and also became a member of the 'Commission for Religious Education in Primary schools'. At each meeting I became the thorn in Mrs. Barnes' side, as I was the lone person questioning the change of curriculum, and prevented the group (by my presence) from being able to unanimously pass a vote to do away with our Bible based Curriculum.

I had come back from many a meeting totally exhausted, and the last meeting I had been to I had an Anglican Bishop sitting opposite me in all his pomp and ceremony: magnificent purple robes and many chains around his neck and rings on his fingers. I assumed he was there to 'keep the peace', and I was so suitably intimidated that I could hardly lift my cup of tea to my lips, let alone squeak out any comments.

Now, here was my daughter suggesting it was time to make a chocolate cake for Mrs. Barnes – the lady who was heading up each of these groups, and who was constantly amazed that I was turning up on each committee. That meant only one thing: Forgive and Bless. Andrea obviously expected me to put a verse into practice we had previously learnt …

"If your enemy is hungry give him food to eat. If he is thirsty give him water to drink – in doing this you will heap burning coals on his head and the Lord will reward you." Proverbs 25:21,22 (KJV).

To make matters worse she was now humming another verse I had taught her years before, *"...and be ye kind one unto another, tender hearted, forgiving one another, even as God for Christ's sake has forgiven you." Ephesians 4.32*

Andrea knew the fight was over. The various committees had finally agreed to allow a choice of curriculum, but it had been a hard time, and I had quite obviously made an enemy because of my outspoken behaviour.

As I watched that glint in my daughter's eye I knew I had no choice.

So the chocolate cake was made and iced. Before the next meeting, with my heart pounding, I quietly tiptoed into Mrs. Barnes' office and carefully placed the cake on her desk with a nice little note of apology and blessing. I was *so* relieved that she was not in her office at the time, and the huge load of relief I felt as I walked from her room was something I will never forget. I had actually done something nice for my enemy. I wondered if she would think I had poisoned the cake!

Just before our final meeting commenced, Mrs. Barnes quietly brushed past my seat and laid a hand on my shoulder. "Thank you for the cake Jan," she whispered with a smile. Suddenly, months of meetings, discussions and arguments vanished in my mind as a special peace overcame me. All was forgiven, and, thanks to my daughter, I had been able to initiate the change in our relationship.

Once again God's way had worked!

There are times when we are required to be tough, to stand up for what we feel is right, but there are also times to move on, and God was now enabling me to move on through the suggestion and timely reminder of my daughter.

From Parent to Parent

Yes, God has suggestions for every situation we may find ourselves in, and answers to every problem we will ever face. As we teach our children – be prepared! They in turn will come back and teach us!

As our children have left home there have been many times when I have asked for their advice, knowing they are each full of godly wisdom and common sense. This is because they are each *full* of God's Words, and, by the time they reached adulthood, Andrea, Jonny, and Michelle had learnt between two and three hundred verses in music, and had been trying to put the principles into practice throughout their childhood.

Now, with so many of these principles being made available to us through Merry, and now her daughter Carolyn, you too can have the privilege of being told what to do by *your* children! Fair's fair after all!

Chapter 18:

To Gossip or not to Gossip

"Where no wood is there the fire goeth out and where there is no tale bearer the strife ceaseth."

Proverbs 26:20 (KJV) Children Arise Volume 5

"Do not let any unwholesome talk come out of your mouth, but only what is helpful for building others up according to their needs, that it may benefit those who listen and do not grieve the Holy Spirit of God with whom you were sealed for the day of redemption."

Ephesians 4:29-30 (KJV) (Unrecorded)

Wow! Beautiful diamonds! Rubies! Sapphires! Pearls! Emeralds!

As my hands were busily sewing a dress for Michelle, I found myself watching what could only be called a vision. Many, many beautiful jewels sparkled in my imagination. Suddenly a thought was spoken quietly into my heart. "Every verse you teach your children will be just as if I am giving them one of these beautiful jewels to keep for ever." I knew what I had received was a thought and a picture straight from God, and I was in awe of what I was seeing.

I had been feeling a little discouraged, and wondering whether I should continue to teach our teenagers Scripture through music. If I did, I knew it would have to be in a slightly more sophisticated form than the 'Verse Times' we had had when they were younger.

I would now remember and be encouraged by this vision for the next ten years as I made the decision that day to continue teaching our children through their teenage years.

So now the challenge was, "how to teach teenagers?" I guess the pattern was already well in place. We had always had afternoon tea and a chat in the lounge room after school, so I made a decision as I sat sewing that day that we would continue to do the same through the High School years, and hopefully the College years as well.

However, instead of me formally teaching a Bible verse as I had in the past, we would learn a new verse in song and mainly just sing it, discussing it casually over afternoon tea and working out how it could be applied in our lives. By now I was very much a Team Member, as I was just as keen to apply these Scriptures in my own life as I was to encourage our teenagers to apply them in theirs.

We had all seen so many family miracles happen as we had sung and applied Scriptures over the years that my sheer enthusiasm probably stopped the children from complaining. The habit had been established, and they were so used to it, that the subtle change from teaching to just singing and a small informal discussion at the end of our fifteen minutes seemed quite acceptable.

One of our first 'teenage verses' was found in Proverbs 26:20. *"Where no wood is there the fire goeth out and where there is no tale bearer the strife ceaseth."*

To complement this verse, and to help us all remember the importance of positive words, we discovered another verse in Ephesians 4: 29 - 30. *"Do not let any unwholesome talk come out of your mouth, but only what is helpful for building others up according to their needs, that it may benefit those who listen and do not grieve the Holy Spirit of God with whom you were sealed for the day of redemption."*

The above verse became one of our favourites before Jonny went off to University to train as a High School Teacher. By now Andrea was married, and Jonny and Michelle were still applying more of God's principles in their lives. We sang this verse so many afternoons that the words had a huge influence on both Jonny and Michelle. Both of them, to this day, find it nearly impossible to gossip and pass on any negative information about others.

Me? I just love to talk! As I write this I can picture the children all nodding their heads in complete agreement! However, sometimes it can lead to gossip. No. Really? Before Michelle left home to get married I still remember regaling the family one day with a juicy story about our neighbour's recent marriage break-up. I didn't notice Michelle's disapproving looks until a voice suddenly piped up.

"Mum! Do not let *any* unwholesome talk come out of your mouth!"

"Whoops!" Sorry Michelle – I'd done it again! Why did some people, like myself, find it so much harder not to gossip than others?

From Parent to Parent.

As I continued to teach through those teen years I began to realize that most young adults learn skills to help them get a good job, but it is the emotional growth and godly character development that is so important to their future success as young adults.

Today, in our society, there is so much wrong that is acceptable, and it is more important than ever that we as parents teach our teenagers, and learn for ourselves, what is right and wrong. To re-establish God's absolutes in our families! But... be prepared! Remember that after a few years of teaching, your children will turn around and begin to teach YOU, and everyone else too!

Andrea teaches her eight children as she Home-Schools them, Jonny is a High School teacher, and Michelle has trained as a Primary School teacher. Teaching comes very naturally to each of them, but most of all they each *love* to teach God's Word to others. We can now agree that those many, many 'Verse times' were so worth it. Be encouraged! Arise parents! Take your rightful place as the teacher and trainer of your children in God's ways and your rewards will be great!

Chapter 19:

The Teenage Counsellor

"Lord Deal with me in loving kindness, and teach me your servant to obey. For I am your servant, therefore give me common sense to apply your words to everything I do."

Psalm 119:124,125. (TLB) Children Arise Vol 5.

"Cast your burdens upon the Lord and He shall sustain thee. He shall never suffer the righteous to be moved."

Psalm 55;22 (KJV) Children Arise Vol 2

Michelle's cheeks had a rosy glow. She had just arrived home from a counselling session with a good friend. She was doing what she loved to do, discipling, counselling and caring.

"Mum," she said "I had to tell Chris that she needed to forgive and bless her parents. I gave her a set of verses to read and made her pray for them!" Michelle was regularly receiving flowers and nice thank you notes and cards from friends who were receiving her counsel. She was continually directing them to different Scriptures she had learnt and proved. At seventeen, she was spending hours each week counselling and praying with many teenage girl-friends who were still like baby Christians as they tried to do life without God's help. The 'Sorting Out Prayer' was being handed out constantly!

At that time she began to say "I'm going to marry a Pastor one day!" She was certainly in training to be a Pastor's wife!

Michelle had been memorizing and practicing Scripture since she was a toddler, and, when we discovered the wonderful verse above, as a family, we began to ask God to give us wisdom and common sense to apply His Words to any problems we encountered.

As we began to thank God for HIS wisdom and common sense, it seemed that Michelle was being given a special dose, as her friends were wanting her advice or opinion on all aspects of their turbulent teenage lives. Michelle had a real God consciousness from a very young age. She was only a baby when our 'Verse times' began and 'the songs' were a part of her life right from the beginning.

It was a natural progression for her then, to want to help all her girlfriends learn to do the same. She had such a heart of care for these girls that, for the last four years, she had her mother rising at 6.30a.m so we could pray for them. Michelle had such a huge heart of compassion that she would feel responsible for her friends, and was willing to put in whatever time was necessary to sort them all out and try to fix their problems.

Towards the end of her year 11, having just turned seventeen, Michelle found she was loving life so much she was trying to pack far too much into it.

Michelle composing in our lounge room

Michelle watching her composition being performed

What exactly was being packed into our teenager's life?

Music was a huge part of Michelle's life. One of the main subjects she had taken that year was music. As Paul and I sat in an end of year concert with other parents, in a lovely old Chalmers church, my mouth opened in astonishment. I listened to a beautiful little group of talented musicians playing a complicated piece of music written by our Michelle! As musicians played violins, cello, clarinet and flute, Michelle accompanied on piano, and Paul and I were totally amazed that all these months of hearing Michelle working out various tunes on our piano at home were now culminating in this amazing piece of music!

There were two more compositions, again with many instruments, and a lovely song sung by her cousin, Carolyn, and accompanied by Michelle. As we walked out of that concert I felt as though I was the mother of a famous composer.

I had no idea our daughter had such a gift of music. I knew that Michelle had been singing all her life, and each of our children had been given piano lessons for as long as they wanted to play. Both Andrea and Michelle had taken their lessons to the Grade 8 standard. Now I felt God was rewarding us for all those lessons as I discovered Michelle was so very passionate about her music. During that year she had also begun to put her own Scriptures to music, and she was becoming a prolific writer of Praise and Worship songs.

This year was also the year that Michelle had decided to help organise a Christian group in the lunch hour for fellow College Students. There was a weekly meeting to organise 'the meeting', and the actual meeting itself was a huge success. It naturally provided Michelle with more friends with problems to share, so more of her time was taken up in that way.

By this stage in Michelle's life our Church Youth Group was also quite a large group, and Friday afternoons found Michelle and her friends cooking supper with me for the thirty or forty young people who were now coming to our home each week. It had become 'the place to BE', and many of the young people were also regulars to tea on a Friday night, so we were on duty from about 4.00 pm till midnight each Friday.

Michelle was very involved in our Church program as well that year, and Sunday mornings and evenings found her at Church, again caring for people. She was also given the opportunity that year to become one of our main worship leaders and pianists.

Her part-time jobs included working at a local shoe shop on Saturdays, and selling Avon products through catalogues.

As I said, Michelle loved life so much she was determined to fit into it as much as she possibly could.

The day came when she succumbed to a bout of glandular fever for a full month.

This was unheard of for Michelle. She could no longer do anything! Instead she had to stay in bed for a whole month! This was one of the biggest teenage trials she had to face. No people! No fun! No program! Just REST!

She finally had to step back from the lives of her friends, and see which ones were now mature enough in themselves to care for her for a change. It was a hard, upsetting, frustrating time for Michelle who had to learn through this experience that the problems her friends experienced were *not her* problems after all. She had to let go and let God sort them out. It was a time of much soul-searching, and many tears.

While some of her many friends were caring and kind many others ignored her completely when she no longer had time for them

During this time of convalescence she came to realize that the words were true in Psalm 119: 124,125

"Lord deal with me in loving kindness and teach me your servant to obey. For I am your servant therefore give me common sense to apply your words to everything I do."

One of the words she now needed to apply was Grandma's special verse in Psalm 55:22. "*Cast your burden upon the Lord and He shall sustain thee. He shall never suffer the righteous to be moved.*"

She realised that, in learning to obey God and His promptings to care for others, she actually had to use her God-given common sense and recognise that ALL needs and problems were not necessarily HER responsibility. As we meditated on the words of these verses and sang them, Michelle resolved to find a better balance in caring for herself as well as caring for her many friends.

In some instances her friends did not really want to change – they just loved all the extra attention and time they were receiving from Michelle.

Through this very hard month of recovery, Michelle decided to listen to God's promptings a little more closely, and learn when to stop and give herself some time and attention, instead of *all* time and attention being lavished on her many friends. She put some boundaries into her life, and learned it was okay to say NO!

Today, as a young adult Michelle still has a big heart for the less fortunate, the grieving and the sick. She enjoys caring for her own children and caring for people in the church where her husband Joe is in training to become… a Pastor!

From Parent to Parent

The stories of the Youth Group in our home are told in the recently produced book 'Teenagers Arise'.

Chapter 20:

The Stolen Car

"Don't worry about anything, instead pray about everything. Tell God your needs and don't forget to thank Him for His answers. If you do this you will experience God's peace which is far more wonderful than the human mind can understand. His peace will keep your thoughts and your heart quiet and at rest as you trust in Christ Jesus."

Philippians: 4:6-7 (TLB) Children Arise Volume 1

"What is faith? It is the confident assurance that something we want is going to happen, it is the certainty that what we hope for is waiting for us even though we cannot see it up ahead."

Hebrews 11:1 (KJV) Children Arise Volume 4

It was unbelievable. Jonny's car had gone! Not just Jonny's car, but it had most of his wardrobe in it too. His favourite T-shirts and jeans, his text books, assignments and study books for Uni, his beloved skateboard, his wetsuit for surfing at the local beach in between Uni classes and his toiletries for the next week away from home.

His old blue Holden Gemini station wagon wasn't worth much, but at the age of twenty-one it was his biggest treasure, and his only means of transport to Hobart for Uni and back at weekends to run the Youth Group in our home on Friday evenings. Jonny also organised a band night at Church once a month on a Sunday night for 80-100 enthusiastic young people, and was lead singer and guitarist in the local band GRRRR, in which he practically shouted (sang?) Scripture he had now put to his own style of music. (He had converted many

Children Arise songs to teenage rock and rap.) Along with his cousin, Alister, and a couple of other mates, Jonny loved singing and playing. And the kids loved Jonny! Their album, GRRRR, was doing the rounds of the local Christian churches, and the boys had quite a following of young people at this time. Nine years later their following has increased.

Many of these young people were at Church this particular Sunday night. Church had just concluded, and the young people were talking and laughing when Jonny came running in with the news.

"My car's gone!" he yelled.

The young people raced outside to look, and sure enough, where Jonny's old blue car had been parked outside the church there was now just an empty, forlorn looking space.

Paul and I had raced out with the young people, and now we stood there in shock. As Jonny's mum I was filled with dismay – whatever would he do without his transport to Hobart? He had been all set to go back to Uni, a two-and-a-half hour trip by car, and his first subject at Uni was at 8.00 a.m the next morning. He would need his assignments and text books, not to mention his change of clothes for each day. This wardrobe travelled back and forth each weekend along with all his other treasures. As I watched the reactions of shock and horror on the faces of his mates I was amazed to see how calm Jonny himself was.

"Quick." he said, "Let's all pray!"

So, while we all bowed our heads he sent up a hurried faith filled prayer that he would find his car with everything intact, and he thanked God that this would be the case.

Then, without wasting any time, he grabbed some mates and went rushing out into the night to cruise around the area in a mate's car, and, eventually, to inform the police.

Having set the example for us all we continued to pray, while young people drove their cars around the city and into some of the roughest suburbs searching for an old blue station wagon. An hour or so later they all returned, and solemnly filed inside with gloomy looks on their faces. Jonny's car was nowhere to be found!

I was still amazed at his calmness and quiet assurance that he would get it back!

I decided a mother has a lot more trouble trusting God for her son's car than her son has for the return of his own car!

Certainly Jonny had practiced Hebrews 11.1 enough times in the past to feel confident that, if we asked, then God could return his car.

It was as though the moment we agreed together and asked God, Jonny had his answer. I could see the other young people were also amazed that he wasn't panicking. His complete peace and calmness was not *normal* to them at all! In fact it looked as though we had just stepped into a test of faith for our whole church, not just for our family.

Fortunately that night another Uni student was travelling back to Hobart, so Jonny waved us off as he caught a lift, minus his books, clothes etc.

The next day as I again pictured Jonny's reaction, I realized he had immediately put Philippians 4:6-7 into practice and it had been an automatic reaction.

"Philippians, 4.4-8. Don't worry about anything, instead pray about everything. Tell God your needs and don't forget to thank Him for His answers. If you do this you will experience God's peace which is far more wonderful than the human mind can understand, His peace will keep your thoughts and your hearts quiet and at rest as you trust in Christ Jesus." (Children. Arise Vol 1)

The instant result for him was peace, and, as we spoke to him on the phone the next day, he was *still* refusing to worry…at all!

"Don't worry Mum!" he said, "I'll get it back. I'm not worried!"

Well! My first reaction was to worry!

What about transport to Uni?

What about all his clothes?

What about his beloved and expensive skateboard?

What about all his Uni textbooks, notes, and assignments?

So Philippians 4:6-7 was an automatic response for Jonny but not yet for his mum.

However, if Jonny really believed his car was coming back, then Paul and I would pray and trust God along with him and I would try to put those horrible niggling thoughts aside.

Two days after the theft Paul and I had just had dinner and were praying about the return of the car. Suddenly Paul sprang up, full of faith, and said "I'm going to look for it! I'm going to drive around some suburbs and see if I can find it!" Then he said, "Pray with me that God will lead me to the right suburb to find it." We had just finished praying when the phone rang.

"Mr. Targett?" It was a policeman. "We think we have located your son's car. It's sitting in a dead end street in Mayfield, and it looks like everything is intact – there are a lot of clothes in it and even a skate-board and a wetsuit!" He answered Paul's prayer by giving the exact instructions on the location of the car.

An hour or so later, when Paul returned with a huge smile all over his face, we phoned Jonny to tell him the amazing news. The car was fine! And there was nothing missing apart from his toiletry bag. His expensive skateboard, almost his entire wardrobe, and his entire library of Uni text books and notes, as well as his expensive wet suit, were all sitting exactly where he had packed them. His unlocked car sat waiting for him in a nearby suburb!

What a miracle. There must have been an angel watching over them. Jonny's first comment when he heard was, "I knew I would get it back! You know that verse Mum? Don't worry about ANYTHING!"

Well! I had twenty years of worry habits to undo, so my first thoughts had been worry! It would be a while longer before I would be able to be like Jonny, and automatically react God's way.

Jonny had *refused* to worry, and instead insisted we all *pray.* I had taught him the verse – now he was teaching his Mum!

As we thanked God that night for His miracle, I realised Jonny had stepped straight into a place of faith and trust completely automatically. He had been an example to his friends and family, and God had rewarded him for that trust.

From Parent to Parent

Our son Jonny taught Paul and I a lot through this experience. Sometimes our children by-pass us as they learn to put God's Words into practice, and, in the area of faith, Jonny certainly by-passed his mother. I was so proud of his example through that difficult time.

Because Jonny was now a prolific song writer and lead singer in his band, GRRRR, he had a huge following of young people, who were all waiting to see what his reaction would be to this catastrophe. He passed that test far better than his mother would have done, and it was incredibly encouraging to see how strong his faith was when it was really put to the test.

The style of music our children love is not always our style as parents, and, while Paul and I sometimes had to wear ear plugs to Jonny's band appointments we always made sure we were there (some times the *only* parents) as we believed in him so much, and were so proud of the songs he wrote and sang.

Parents, we don't know the results of that time we spend teaching our children until they are tested in some way. Let's not wait until the test before we try to teach them. Let's have them as well prepared for life as we possibly can!

Jonny singing with his band Grrrr

Chapter 21:

And Finally...

It was now the last week in August. The week my assignment was drawing to a close.

The last week of the final month I had been given to have these stories written down!

Every morning for five days our CD player turned itself on at exactly 9.15 a.m, and the Children Arise C.D (left there for the grandchildren) began to play! It played for fifteen minutes and then stopped.

Please ask my husband Paul if you don't believe this, as my family know I can lean towards the dramatic!

Paul heard it too.

By the third morning Paul asked if I had turned on the CD player. I explained that it was playing by itself each morning. His logical brain assumed that it must have been somehow set to turn on. This continued every morning for those final five days of writing, and, apart from that week, and the one time that I mentioned it had happened in chapter one, it has not happened before or since.

"Thank you God! I accept your confirmation that, as other parents needed to hear the Scriptures in music through the Children Arise CDs – now they need to hear the stories behind the songs!

Was it worthwhile spending the time to make sure our children knew how to *do* what each Scripture said? Yes! A thousand times Yes!

These stories are for *today*! They have been written to give you, fellow parent, HOPE in bringing up your children in God's ways.

As I write this final chapter I am sitting in our lounge room watching the sun rise in the sky above the beautiful Tamar River. Birds are just beginning to chirp and a new day is dawning.

As I watch the awesome sight of the sun rising to a brand new day, my prayer is that you too, my fellow reader and parent, will ARISE! and begin your own adventure with your own precious family.

From Parent to Parent

Today, as I write thc conclusion to 'Parents Arise', Paul and I have two of our grandchildren staying in our home for a week, as our daughter Michelle has just given birth to her beautiful third child, Esther Louise Duffy.

As I concluded my last sentence and put down my pen I heard Samuel (two) crying loudly from his bedroom. Caitlyn (three and a half) woke up and together we went in to see Samuel.

"Fwwwwiiiii!" He wailed loudly. "Fwwwwiiiii!!"

Caitlyn and brother Samuel

"He's scared of that fly!" Caitlyn interpreted. She immediately took charge as only Caitlyn can. "Sam," she crooned in a sweet voice, "you don't have to be afraid of flies! Remember the verse?"

Sammy stopped crying and stared at her. "Remember?" she lisped, "*God has not given us a thpirit of fear but of love and of power and of a thound mind!* So Thammy!" She emphasized with her little finger pointing at him, "*God has not given YOU a thpirit of fear, but of power and of love and of a thound mind.* See? So YOU don't have to be thcared anymore!

You don't have to be afwaid of fwies (flies) or bugs or even thpiders!"

As she enthusiastically gestured to the fly and then pointed her little finger back at Sammy, I laughed with delight as I realized that, just as God had set her free from her own huge fear of flies, flying bugs and spiders, through the verse Michelle had taught her (2 Timothy 1:7), now at the age of three Caitlyn was already teaching her little brother to apply God's Words to his own little life as a toddler.

Parent: As soon as your child can sing, they can be learning the Scripture through songs! Michelle has been playing 'the Songs' to Caitlyn since she was a baby. She now knows every verse on five CDs. and is already beginning to put God's Words into practice. It is never too early to begin!

(Paul and I would love to hear from you as you begin your own adventure.)

Resources

Parents Arise - Raising Children God's Way Course on DVD (six sessions)

Parents Arise - Raising Children God's Way Manual

Uncle Paul's Story Book (12 selected stories to help teach 12 Scripture verses to children.)

Verse Time activity books – coming soon!

Children Arise C.D. volume 1

Children Arise C.D. volume 2

Children Arise C.D. volume 3

Children Arise C.D. volume 4

Children Arise C.D. volume 5

Children Arise music book for volume 1 and 2

Children Arise music book for volume 3 and 4

Teenagers Arise - book

For orders and further information please contact Paul and Janine Targett on:

Website: www.parentsarise.com.au

Email: janine@parentsarise.com.au

Email: paul@parentsarise.com.au

CPSIA information can be obtained
at www.ICGtesting.com
Printed in the USA
BVIC01n0759291015
3407BVAU00005B/7